*You Can Do Better!*

### Declan Byrnes

### Management Coach & Biography

**Declan specialises** in helping individuals to analyse their current role and effectiveness, to identify and complete improvement actions for better individual impact and contribution to the business. Declan also provides coaching to managers to clarify organisation and business problems, to identify action priorities and objective help to deal with them.

Declan graduated from Trinity College Dublin in 1980 with an honours degree in Organic Chemistry. From 1980 onwards throughout his career the Abbott Corporation employed him, which is a large Fortune 500, US multinational healthcare company.

Declan has held a diverse range of roles during his 26.5 years with Abbott including...

Quality Supervisor; Quality Engineer; Production Supervisor; Process Engineer; Process Engineering Manager; Product Development Manager; and Customer Liaison Manager.

## *You Can Do Better!*

For the 2nd half of his career he held 4 diverse senior management posts as Business Unit Manager of 2 different business units and also held roles as Quality Manager and Materials/Part Engineering Manager. He has travelled widely in Europe, the United States and Japan. As a result Declan has gained varied and diverse operations, business and people management experience throughout his career. He has shown particular interest in self and employee development. He has trained and learned from many management programmes over the years including Abbott in house and Cranfield School of Management senior management development courses. In 2006 he was awarded an MSc in Management Practice from Trinity College Dublin/Irish Management Institute. Since 2007 he has been working as a freelance management consultant and coach.

*You Can Do Better!*

## Index of Contents  Page No.

*You Can Do Better!*

## Index of Contents                                              Page No.

4

*You Can Do Better!*

**Index of Contents**                                             **Page No.**

*You Can Do Better!*

*You Can Do Better!*

## Foreword and Introduction

**This book** is a very practical tool and a self-development aid for individuals who aspire to be better at what they do. It will also benefit business owners and people who have responsibility for others within organisations, both small and large. Individuals in a business or organisation share a common purpose, that of self-managing and self-acting to be effective. Remember even if you are not a manager of people you need to be a good self–manager and interact well with others to be a success. This book is valuable to these individuals as it covers a lot of everyday practical material on self-development, personal leadership, dealing effectively with others and other important work behaviours. Working with this book will increase your self-knowledge and understanding thus helping to widen your horizons. It will add to your repertoire of knowledge and practical skills giving you greater ability and flexibility to respond to issues and challenges, thus making you more useful to your business.

There are 10 modules in all and each is prefaced with a short outline to set the context for what follows in the module. The book can be used in an "a la carte" fashion and you can dip in and out of various parts as you wish and on what you find relevant and important. Hence there is no need to slavishly follow the order of the book.

### *You Can Do Better!*

Module 3, Qualities of an Effective Individual and Manager, is one core section of the book which deals with the individual, and manager and effective behaviours for managing yourself, your work and where it applies, managing others. This is central to the book and hence I have gone into some detail to expand on points made to clarify for you the intended behaviours by using practical examples in many cases.

To emphasise the practical nature of the book action plans are provided with each of the behaviours and you can use these actions as a basis to work on identified improvement and development areas.

You are invited to complete the questionnaire at the end of the book. It is straightforward to fill out and score and is intended to give an insight into your strengths and identify self and general management areas in which you could improve. Just answer the questions that apply to you based on your own role. You could also ask colleagues to complete the questionnaire for you, compare results and thus illuminate differences between your self-perception and how others view you. Finally after an appropriate time lapse and development has taken place you are invited to repeat completing the questionnaire and track what progress you have made on your personal development in the meantime.

As individuals and managers we apply routines or models in our working day on what we have found to work by experience. This is because dealing with

*You Can Do Better!*

others and people management is not an exact science and hence essentially all individuals and managers consciously (or sub-consciously) use behavioural models of what works to get by. This book addresses the common and the not so common behavioural models as they are applied in practice. The book assumes you are technically competent and proficient in your role and is thus targeted to improving your self-management, self-development, your interactions with people and where/when it applies your general management of people. The focus is on the individual practitioner and what you can do to be more effective. The approach is on the practical, i.e. what you can do in everyday work situations using models and ways of thinking to improve your impact and your contribution to the business. For simplicity I have used the masculine, he for the individual or manager - equally well it could be she as is often the case in practice.


"*I used to be conceited but now I know I'm perfect*" is both a witty and useful saying. It introduces the idea of performance excellence, something we aspire to as individuals and managers of work and managers of people, but never quite reach. We are all on a continuous development journey and we are each one of us a work in progress in God's eyes. The effective individual is well aware and conscious of his own development journey and is proactive in its progress ultimately aspiring towards individual performance excellence. Always remember – *You Can Do Better!*

### *You Can Do Better!*

Having gone through the book you may feel that you could never hope to attain all the good qualities and behaviours mentioned. This may be true and therefore you should be thinking of continuous improvement for yourself, which is doable rather than delayed perfection, which may never come. In other words, work with what you find useful and try to work it into your routine practice to help make you a more effective individual and manager of work and/or of people. Of course you may not agree with some of the suggested approaches or they may not be relevant or suit your situation. That's OK, ignore them and focus on what you find useful and can apply.

My goal is that this book will help you to stop and really think about your current role, your effectiveness, and what improvement and development needs you have as you progress along with your job and career. My hope is that some of what I say in this book will inspire you to go and *Do Better!* Finally, my very best wishes go to you as you set out to better yourself, increase your contribution and progress your career.

## Module 1     First Things

**To begin** I think it is important to consider the initial questions for you as they relate to self and people management. The first and most obvious question is how much of yourself are you prepared to give to your job and to your career. The answer to this question is important as there needs to be a clear match between the commitment and energy that you as an individual and/or as a manager are prepared to give and the ambition level you hold for your career. Having dealt with your own commitment the next important question clearly needs to be asked of those who may report to you and what they can bring to the job.

Not so obvious is the next question of Emotional Intelligence or the more common term of interpersonal skills and your ability and development in this area. *How good you are here, will dictate how well you get on with people, how much you can get done both along with and through people and ultimately how effective and successful you can be in your career.* Despite technology advances working lives seem to be getting busier and busier with personal discretionary time under increasing pressure. Hence the notion of time management and its most effective use is an important one. The concept of self-development and of taking personal responsibility for your own development is a major factor in making successful progress in your career.

Finally, your behavioural style and appropriate fit with the culture of your organisation is an important issue worth consideration and is discussed briefly.

## 1.1 Commitment & Ambition

How much commitment do you have for your current role and what ambition do you have for your future career? How much time and energy are you prepared to expend on an on-going basis on your job?

What defines you? What are your views on work-life balance and your other non-career priorities e.g. relationships with spouse/partner, children, family and friends, hobbies and interests? More accurately perhaps how much work-life imbalance are you prepared to tolerate?

What do you want from life? - do you want to do more, be more, have more or maybe you are happy with your current lot? What ideally do you want to be, do and have in life? Prioritise your ideals in terms of what you profoundly need rather than what you want and then work on putting the theoretical ideals into actual practice transforming them into values with significant meaning for you. One good definition of success is that you achieve what you value. This begs the question of you – sort out what you value.

It is vital that you have asked yourself and answered questions like the above to know what you want, what you are prepared to do and as important what you are not prepared to do.

The bottom line is that what results from your decisions on life priorities will decide the level of commitment you ultimately give to your job and career. In short there needs to be congruency between your ambition and what commitment you are prepared to put behind it. By the by, there are those who feel swamped by their career as if it was out of their hands. In reality these people are being passive and are allowing others to dictate the pace. Everyone of course, must give a certain minimum commitment to their job to be reasonably effective but beyond that it really is your own choice as to how much more of yourself and personal commitment you are both able and want to give. Stating the obvious then, the greater your ambition the greater your commitment must be to your job and career. High commitment demands high energy from you and exclusive focused attention on your self-development and career progression plans.

## 1.2 Aim High - It's Up to You!

Frequently you can come across business owners and higher managers speaking about some of their people in a disappointed fashion thinking that they will never progress much further due to some limiting factors and because "that's just the way he is". The question for you in any weaknesses or shortcomings you may have is are you going to be passive on it, i.e. *"that's just the way I am"* **or** are you going to take a more proactive approach, Aim High and think, *"I will be who I decide to be"*. So the choice is yours, proactive or

13

passive, Aim High or Low? – It's up to You! .Always remember – *You Can Do Better!*

## 1.3 Contribution = Willing + Able

If you are a manager you are likely to have a number of people reporting to you. Each individual report makes a specific contribution to the business, which can be simply described as the summation of their willingness and ability to do the job. (Note: Contribution is further defined in some detail in Module 4). Your job as a manager of people is to create the circumstances in which each individual's contribution is optimised. That being said, it is the responsibility of each individual concerned (and not the manager's) to work on and improve his or her own contribution. It is essential to understand that it is up to the employee to decide to kick the ball (or not) and how hard to kick it – with the manager acting as a conduit to performance.

2 further general points are worth making at this stage,

    (a) The manager can make significant progress with individuals who are willing but less able by e.g. coaching them, training them etc. It is a lot more difficult with unwilling employees to increase their contribution unless their commitment is somehow regained which generally comes from within them.

(b) The manager needs to be proactive in developing his people notwithstanding the qualifications made above. He needs to improve and optimise his people's contribution, as ultimately his performance will be a reflection of how effective his people are in completing their roles.

## 1.4 Emotional Intelligence

*"You can never become to be what you can be until you first accept who you are"* is I think a very important and powerful quotation. For me this means you need to understand and accept yourself for whom you are, control and manage yourself and have an accurate assessment of your strengths and shortcomings.

Leading on from this, it is critical then that you have the motivation, self-knowledge and self-esteem needed to confront and remedy your weaknesses, and of course playing to your strengths thus increasing your overall effectiveness. This is best encapsulated along with other interpersonal traits and skills in the theory of Emotional Intelligence on which subject there are numerous books and articles written. (e.g. Understanding Emotional Intelligence by Daniel Goleman and numerous Harvard Business Review articles.)

At its simplest emotional intelligence consists of;

- Self-awareness

- Self-regulation

- Motivation

- Empathy and

- Social skills,

Self-awareness is probably most important as a starting position for you. Each of the five elements above is further subdivided into a framework of practical traits, personal and interpersonal skills and another reference to this is the Hay framework of emotional intelligence. Not to put too fine a point to it apart from having a good technical knowledge of your job, (which would be a basic requirement for your role) the second most important thing you can do in your career is to develop strong interpersonal skills. A very good vehicle for this is to understand and learn about emotional intelligence and all its facets and put what you have understood and learned into everyday practice. It is my firm belief that embracing emotional intelligence, understanding yourself, developing and mastering your personal and interpersonal skills is a critical success factor for today's individual and business manager.

## 1.5 Time Management

I'll keep this short because I don't have the time! Ha! What you can get done and achieve in a day is down to you, i.e. time management is really about self-management. When you come into the office or workplace in the morning nobody puts a gun to your head and tells you what you are going to do for the rest of the day. Nobody forces you to pick up the ringing telephone, to read that interesting (but unimportant and distracting) e-mail, to attend the meeting on some peripheral subject, (even though you have pressing priorities) to have idle banter with numerous colleagues etc. The key message is to take charge of your own time and don't let others hijack it and take charge of it. So, time to focus! Establish and reset priorities daily and concentrate your work and attention around them each day. Lift your head up every now and then and be 'human', interact and relate with your colleagues. Take appropriate breaks to refresh yourself. Also when you are a manager of people always keep time available to listen to them, be patient, help and direct them as needed and build rapport. The trick is to balance your personal priorities with your time for colleagues and for managing people. This demands that you control yourself and your time very effectively and never fill up your day thus leaving time capacity to deal with the unexpected and to action priorities. You leave work primarily when you are satisfied with the number of ticks against your daily priorities - the actual time of day you leave is secondary to this.

## 1.6 Self-Management & Development

There is only one person responsible for your development - that's you - yourself! One time when I asked a sometimes-witty Engineer to do some pressing job for me he replied by saying he would put his best man on it! I was impressed. You need to put your best man on your own self-management and development. Self-management is about being self-reliant and acting independently, using your own resources and initiative and quite a bit of it has to do with being proactive on improving your own mental maturity and understanding. A significant amount of this can be gained by increasing your knowledge and practice of emotional intelligence, which has previously been discussed.

The development piece I think largely comes from experiential (on the job) learning, being open to a wide range of experiences, which helps you to learn, develop and grow as an individual. Experience helps you to respond more effectively to pressures and events and ultimately contribute more as time goes on. The more roles and diversity you encounter your range of experiences will be greater and hence your learning and development will be broader. An important point to note is that you can deepen your understanding and personal development by reading and reflecting on appropriately targeted material from books, manuals and articles. Finally, you will get development from attending suitable training courses in terms of knowledge that can be imparted but the significant growth for you will come from testing and putting the learning into actual practice. So it's up to you! - will you put your best man onto your growth and development?

## 1.7 **Work Culture and your Fit**

Work culture can be defined as "the way things are done around here". Given this definition what impact could work culture have on your role and self-management style? In whatever business and organisation you work in, it will have its own culture its own way of doing things. In tandem with this a predominant behavioural style emerges which is congruent with the culture and with the habits and beliefs of the business managers and the general workforce.

Therefore, a certain range of management behaviours culminating in a management style emerges as being appropriate and acceptable within the organisation. The range of management styles can vary wildly between e.g. open door, informal, participatory and democratic right through to closed door, formal, directive and autocratic. An individual whose self-management style or his style of managing others differs with the predominant style of the business is likely to find it more difficult to be successful and may even be labelled as a maverick and a bit of an outsider. At a minimum, lack of fitting in is likely to be a source of frustration for the individual and perhaps also for the organisation. So the question for you is what are your operating habits and beliefs, what is your self-management style and does it fit in with the culture of your business? If it does not fit then a key question for you is; are you prepared to change to fit? - if not, it will be unlikely or at least significantly more difficult for you to realise your potential within the business.

When talking about cultures I think it's no harm to briefly mention working with people with different national cultures on an international basis. When dealing internationally it is certainly wise and prudent to take the time to understand the basic cultural grounding of whoever you are dealing with. You can do this in advance by asking other informed colleagues or if this does not work then inquire of the people who you are dealing with directly. In most situations people from other cultures will be pleased with your genuine inquiring efforts. They will be glad to let you know how best they would like to deal with you what is important for them in terms of appropriate and effective communications and behaviours and how they would like to be treated in general.

## Module 2     Communications

**Effective individuals**, managers and leaders are good communicators, that allow them to relate well, building rapport with others, which ultimately helps in getting the work of the business done.

Remember its "Results through People" and hence making the necessary connections between people at all levels in the business is a vital part of the process. Communication is a key ingredient in all this and what follow are some pointers in the various modes of communication within an organisation.

### 2.1 Communication and Effective Listening

Listening is a skill that is underused by most people...

Do you listen...?

to talk?

to win?

OR to understand?

The effective individual and manager is a good listener. People know that they can come and talk to him but importantly also that he will take the necessary time and effort to really listen to them and understand them. He will make the extra effort to listen, not to interrupt, and not to assume what the other person is saying, not cutting them off short to reply. In fact he will ask probing questions on occasion to check his understanding of what is said and what the other person wishes to communicate. This method of active listening by asking questions is not easy and requires extra effort from the individual or manager. Clearly it requires him to clear his mind, staying quiet, being patient and focusing all his attention on what the other person is saying and what it means. Effective listening also means not trying to do something else also at the same time - shuffling paperwork, reading etc. Only when the person has said their piece as it were, and that the individual or manager has understood what the person wished to convey can he truly be in an informed position to respond to them.

It is said that there is a risk in really listening to someone - you may have to change your mind!!

Now is the time to begin deliberately talking less and listening more - your behaviour will be noticed and you will be more effective for it.

## 2.2 1-to-1 Meetings

The one to one meeting is the most effective form of communication. This is because it is the best forum for the manager to listen to and understand his people. Also it helps him to understand their needs and their position and to let them know his position and what he needs from them. Given that the 1-to-1 meeting is of a private nature, important and pressing issues can be discussed openly and honestly.

It is said that communication is the creation of understanding. 1-to-1 meetings can be very effective for this very reason, i.e. that both parties, the manager and reportee can reach an understanding of each other, what the goals and priorities are, and what their respective positions on each are.

The format of 1-to-1 meetings is generally as follows;

The meeting is prearranged and is held privately in an office or at least in a quiet place out of earshot of colleagues. The manager will have a draft agenda which he will have previously copied to his report. He leads the meeting going through the agenda item by item checking for progress against goals, taking time to talk through any difficulties and issues which might hinder further progress. Having reviewed each issue fully the manager where needed, will look for a commitment to action on goals and will agree a task schedule with the reportee for follow up in future meetings.

Once the manager is satisfied he has covered all the main issues and is happy with proposed action plans then he should leave the floor, so to speak, to his reportee. The reportee then goes through his own agenda items some of which may have already been covered in their earlier discussion.

Once the reportee is happy that all his agenda items are covered then the manager and reportee can update each other on general items of communications, business news, upcoming events etc. Once this is done the manager will summarise key goals and commitments made against the agreed action items. He then sets up a follow up meeting with his reportee say 2 or 3 weeks into the future or at least far enough into the future to allow plans to develop and progress to be made against agreed commitments. At this juncture the manager can close the meeting.

As in all management situations difficulties are encountered from time to time, goal progress is delayed, unforeseen problems emerge which need solving. The 1-to-1 meeting is an ideal way of dealing with problems and concerns that individuals can have which is hindering progress. On these occasions the manager can advise and coach his people on the way forward. Sometimes this means a change of approach and behaviour by the reportee. The manager can communicate the needed change effectively in the 1-to-1 meeting process using a friendly and non-threatening manner. He can encourage and direct his reportee towards the required behaviour change as needed. Clearly the manager must ensure that his communications are clear and that his expectations of his reportee are clearly stated and understood by the reportee and that it is understood that the expectations will be rigorously followed up as part of future 1-to-1 meetings between them.

Also, by the way, sometimes the reportee may need to convince his manager that goals and action plans need to be changed and hence that the manager's own expectations must be changed.

The 1-to-1 meeting process is a very effective method of communication between the manager and his reports. It is an open and 2 way feedback process and when properly handled and managed builds communication, trust and ultimately rapport between the manager and his people.

## 2.3 Group meetings

The main reasons for holding group meetings are to update everyone on the business position, to obtain a communal progress update against stated objectives and commitments, to discuss issues and concerns arising jointly and to inform and learn about general items and new events.

A key objective also though, for the group meeting for the manager is to build relationships, communal rapport and teambuilding as part of the meeting process, i.e. we are all in this together. Meetings should follow a pre-set agenda with adequate time set aside to discuss all agenda items and making allowances for group discussion. Given that this is a group meeting the manager should generally avoid getting into great detail on any business issue unless it is of a business-critical nature in which case it will warrant significant discussion and debate by the group.

The main thrust of the meeting should be to inform and communicate - problem solving and getting into detail should be dealt with separately from these meetings. The usual rules of meetings management apply, i.e. the manager should coordinate the agenda, gate keep, watch the time and ensure balanced participation from the group members. One final important point is that group meetings have a tendency to have a life of their own and will go on and on if left unchecked. The manager therefore needs to ensure he keeps a tight rein on proceedings, the discussion threads etc., and push for summarising and concluding on discussions so that the group's time is not wasted.

## 2.4 Other modes of communication

### Group Communications

Make sure that you have a clear purpose and clear objectives for the group communication. Communicate to large groups of people as briefly as possible. Stick to the key points and get the intended messages (of which there should be only a few) across. Check for understanding if necessary. Allow for a few questions at the end. Answer the relevant questions briefly. Be careful, - large group meetings have a strong tendency at times to throw up awkward, negative and unhelpful (to the communications process) questions. Answer the questions as honestly and as briefly as you can. Don't get into a debate with the employee who took all year to think up of the most difficult question for you to answer. Close the meeting first and speak as necessary with the individual separately afterwards.

## *You Can Do Better!*

### E–Mail

E-mail is the new version of verbal diarrhoea in electronic form. Develop a system that works for you that filters your e-mails rigorously and allows you to focus only on those e-mails on key and important subjects and/or from key people and clients. You can largely ignore e-mails you are cc'ed on. E-mails which directly impact on you will generally be addressed directly to you. Strictly limit your time to read e-mails and don't let it encroach on your other priority work. As a suggested approach quickly scan your inbox by sender and subject and mark those that need your attention and schedule to read them at an allotted quieter time in your day after you have cleared your priority work.

Some e-mails you compose will be particularly important e.g. a matter of record to a client on some important issue. In such cases take the necessary time to draft and redraft the e-mail carefully until you are happy with the content and the wording before you issue it. If the content is particularly sensitive question whether e-mail is appropriate or whether face-to-face communication may be more appropriate. Keep your own e-mails short and to the point using concise and non-flowery language. Remember unlike a conversation e-mail is a form of permanent record. Hence, in general keep your writing style formal and non-conversational.

## Telephone Conversations

When making a telephone call, remember the rule - relationships 1st and business 2nd. For important calls and ones that you expect to cover a lot of ground, it can be helpful to jot down key topics prior to the call to help you cover all the points you need during the call. Keep an eye on the clock with telephone conversations as they can eat up a lot of your valuable time inadvertently if left unchecked. Remember telephone conversations can only achieve so much, face-to-face conversation is always better.

## 2.5 Communication Highlights

### *"That's Not What I Meant!"*

The meaning of communication is in the response you get. Effective communication happens when what is understood by others matches your intended message. So, be sure to check with the people concerned, for the receipt, correct interpretation and understanding of your message.

### Communication and Attribution

On a similar theme be careful what you attribute to people, i.e. assigning motives to people for the way they are or the way they behave. So don't assume that you know where they are coming from as this approach is lazy and often times you can be wide of the mark. It is better to take the trouble to investigate whatever the issue is with the people directly concerned or if this is not possible then going behind the scenes to more fully understand the situation. Having a more informed and accurate perspective on people puts you in a better position to interact and respond to them more effectively.

## Communication and Conflict

Conflict could be described as a form of communication between people that has gone out of control. In such cases you can de–escalate the conflict to the lesser problem of a disagreement by removing emotion from the situation and the associated undue personal investment in entrenched positions. Once emotion is absent, the position, needs and interests of both parties can be calmly and assertively stated and listened to without pre-judging. From this point on, if you leave personalities aside, the substantive issues can be identified and debated on their merits leading to a negotiated solution acceptable to both parties.

So the obvious question you need to answer is how to remove your emotion from the situation? I suggest you use a 2 Step- Back process. The 1st step back is for you to say to yourself in your mind – "I'm not mad at you (i.e. the other party in the conflict), I'm mad at the issue". The 2nd step back is for you to say in your mind – "In truth I'm not actually mad at the issue, it is just that I don't agree with the interpretation of it". Once you take the 2nd step back then it is easier to step into a more useful debate with the other party leading to a mutual resolution.

Sometimes of course it can be that emotions are particularly heightened in which case it can be difficult if not impossible to "come down" to the required rational debate. In this case I suggest you count down in your mind from 20 to 1 and due to the concentration required in doing this it will free your mind temporarily from the upsetting emotion. Again if this does not work to calm you sufficiently the best strategy is to step away from the situation altogether and return to it only when you're sure that your mind is once again calm and your emotions are in check. This may mean to leave things sit overnight and deal with the situation more effectively the following day – you are likely to find that the other party has calmed down also and is probably anxious to make amends and resolve the issues between both of you.

**Communication and Influencing**

A precondition for influencing others is that you have first built up good communications, rapport and trust with the people over a period. Over time you will have demonstrated personal integrity to them by being open and honest, by following up on any commitments you made, and by clearly matching what you say with what you do. This earns you the trust of people and puts you in a position of influence with them.

*You Can Do Better!*

On the other hand if you have not acted consistently, openly in good faith and with integrity then trust will be absent and any influencing you attempt will be seen as manipulation and is unlikely to be successful.

In summary then, developing influence is built on earned trust which comes from good communications (which includes active listening and being attentive to others' needs and interests), rapport building and always behaving consistently with integrity.

## Communication and Presentations

In my experience presentations tend to be overused and overdone. The more successful presentations tend to be clear on message, concise and to the point with a small number of key messages in total (perhaps 4 – 5). Having sat through many long and often boring presentations (the ones I presented were always excellent in content and delivery of course!) I think that there are a number of guidelines to follow which will help you to do better in this area.

**Need**  - Consider 1$^{st}$ what you are trying to communicate and to whom. It may well be that a round table discussion with a few charts and a summary page may be the better way to get the information across rather than a formal stand-up presentation

Objective – Be clear what you are trying to do e.g.

- Do you just need to impart and communicate information

## *You Can Do Better!*

- Do you want to inform people on new developments for their reflection

- Do you want to promote serious discussion as part of your communication exercise

- Do you need decisions to be taken on your topic

- Do you need to sell something to your audience (yourself, a service or a product)

- Do you want attention because you were ignored as a child (just kidding!)

**Personal Objective** – Clearly sort out in your own mind are you just trying to inform or are you also trying to impress! Answer the question; what does a successful presentation on this occasion mean? (in terms of impact on your audience and their reaction)

**Be Audience Centred** – if you were in their shoes would you be happy to hear about and sit through the presentation as you have outlined it? Don't hijack their time or rob them of their goodwill towards you by padding your information unnecessarily or worse still waffling on about minor issues, points and concerns. Keep the presentation focused and running at a business-like pace. If on the other hand members of the audience want to stop you to talk around issues – let them and when you feel that adequate time has been given for this politely suggest that you move on.

### *You Can Do Better!*

**Content** – Less is More! Keep the number and the actual content of slides/data sheets as small and as concise and summarised as possible. You can then talk around and expand on the key points of each slide. When your audience needs more information they will ask questions which can then lead to useful discussion. If you have a lot of information to impart, consider the use of hand-outs or provide more information electronically.

**Delivery -** The general rule of presentations is that they should be interesting, entertaining and memorable. You need to engage your audience and if possible get them to participate with you in this communications forum. Make sure you have good punchy content and put particular effort into research etc. to come up with new, diverting and fresh approaches. A word of caution here though – make sure your substance is much stronger than your style i.e. less of the fancy slides, colours and gimmicks. Self–deprecation (humour against yourself) is generally a good idea and if you can inject some other mild inoffensive humour into the presentation – do so.

**Personal Style** – Put your personal stamp on the presentation by being eloquent, yet concise. When appropriate share personal opinions, experiences and stories with your audience. Use vivid images and metaphors to get your points across. Show enthusiasm, commitment and personal energy for your subject. Smile at people and look them in the eye on occasion. Try to be

## *You Can Do Better!*

upbeat and as positive as you can, finishing on a positive note. Finally If possible try to enjoy the experience as you go through the presentation as this will be picked up by the audience at a subliminal level and can be helpful to both you and them.

*You Can Do Better!*

Module 3 | **Behaviours of an Effective Individual and Manager**

### PART 1

**What follows** is detail on your 10 core behaviours as an effective individual, manager of work and where appropriate manager of people. Each core behaviour is then taken in turn and broken into sub behaviours and further analysed and where possible examples are given to help clarify and expand on each point where it applies. Taking all behaviours together may be regarded as dealing with the ideal situation, i.e. you are perfect. More realistically, in many business situations the contingency theory applies, i.e. the approach you use will depend on the context of the particular situation, the people involved, the issues etc. Hence you need to pick and choose the appropriate behaviour(s) which best fits the situation in which you find yourself.

All behaviours described below of course can be prefaced by the word – **YOU**

Given the amount of material to be discussed here I have split the 10 behaviours into 3 manageable chunks which you the reader will find easier to digest. So part 1 with 3 behaviours is detailed below, parts 2 (with 4 behaviours) and part 3 (with the 3 final behaviours) are spaced out for more reader comfort in later parts of the book.

## 3.1 WORK TO HIGH STANDARDS

meaning............**YOU.....**

*Are hard working*

*Demand high standards from yourself and your staff*

*Are punctual*

*Meet commitments*

*Set stretching goals and targets for yourself and your people*

*Work hard to eliminate shoddy work and poor work practices*


**Break-Out      3.1 WORK TO HIGH STANDARDS**

### 3.1.1 *Are Hard Working*

Some people punch in long hours at the office (coming in before standard start time and or leaving after standard finish time) and yet are not effective. Why? They think by being there, so-called "presenteeism" somehow adds to their effectiveness. Their motives can also be political in the sense of being seen "to be going the extra mile". (especially if bosses are working long hours too) They somehow manage to fill their long days and undoubtedly pad them with holding and attending unnecessary and overly long meetings, having long chats with colleagues on trivial issues and having numerous overlong social telephone conversations with contacts and generally "shooting the breeze". They work to the premise that I'm here to 7.30pm anyway so I've plenty of time to talk to

Harry about his new golf driver and how it's changing his game. There is a good one-liner by Woody Allen, which says, "80% of success in life is turning up". However there is more to it than this - it's what you do with the time that counts!

Unfortunately all these people are doing is wasting a lot of their own time and probably that of others' also. Put simply, hardworking means focused concentration on making progress on your priorities throughout the day. You leave the office when you feel you have made adequate progress, i.e. your day's work is done and not what the clock says.

Effective hard working people rarely spend just the statutory 8 hours in the office as they are hardworking they are motivated to stay until they have made their self-targeted progress for the day. However, they are self-aware enough to leave before they get tired and effectiveness diminishes and are disciplined enough to leave on or before time on days when particularly effective progress was made. Hard working effective people do attend meetings but tend to limit them and when possible their duration. In other words they don't let other people hijack or waste their time

**ACTION ITEMS**

⇨ *Set and write down your action priorities - daily, weekly and monthly (at the start of each period)*

### *You Can Do Better!*

⇨ *Use concentrated focus on completing your priorities regardless of other potential distractions*

⇨ *Regularly review progress on your priorities (daily, weekly and monthly) line through completed priorities, reset the remaining ones and add new ones*

⇨ *Repeat the cycle*


### 3.1.2 *Demand high standards from yourself and your staff*

Progress is hard-wired into the human condition creating the need for continual learning and development and ultimately progress. One pre-condition for progress is that standards are set high enough that development occurs.

If you adopt low standards you will surely fail.

If you adopt mediocre standards you will never shine and more competent people and organisations will likely surpass you.

If you adopt high standards development is probable and future success is attainable.

Setting the standard bars high creates the need for on-going high performance. This challenges people not only to do as well as they did before but to stretch themselves by continually developing, learning new job/business aspects, being creative and innovative in solving business problems. By stretching themselves they are also pushing out their boundaries of performance and achievement.

*You Can Do Better!*

Progress is a given for survival and hence so is the need for high standards in all work areas.

## ACTION ITEMS

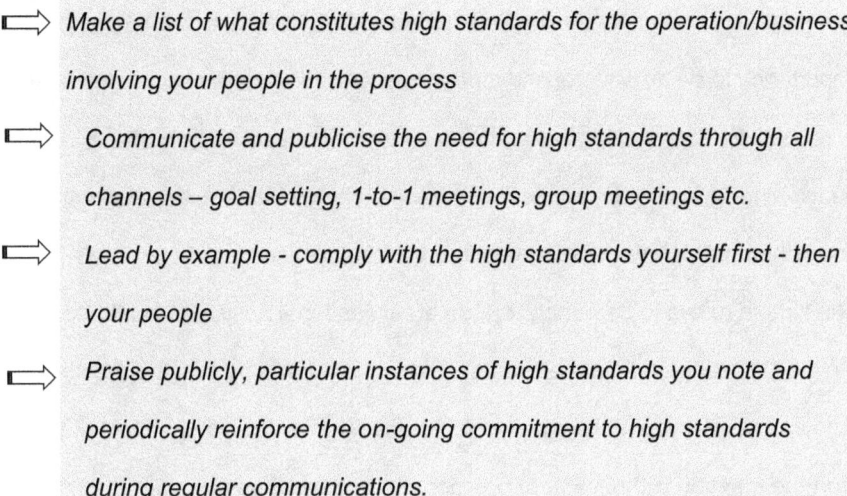

⇒ *Make a list of what constitutes high standards for the operation/business, involving your people in the process*

⇒ *Communicate and publicise the need for high standards through all channels – goal setting, 1-to-1 meetings, group meetings etc.*

⇒ *Lead by example - comply with the high standards yourself first - then your people*

⇒ *Praise publicly, particular instances of high standards you note and periodically reinforce the on-going commitment to high standards during regular communications.*

### 3.1.3 *Are punctual*

You've been asked to attend a scheduled 2-hour meeting starting at 10am. 6 of you arrive early and spend 15 minutes chatting waiting for the other 4 people to arrive. At 10.15 2 more arrive and various calls are made to locate the final 2 participants. The last 2 show up after 10.20 and finally the meeting gets underway at 10.25. You now know you won't make it back to your desk for your next appointment at 12 O'clock. What a waste of everybody's time!

### *You Can Do Better!*

Of all the excuses proffered with respect to late attendance rarely if ever, is the excuse justified, i.e. a life threatening situation, a real emergency or business crisis. (if they genuinely were, chances are they would not have been able to attend the meeting at all) In reality, late attendees simply don't attend meetings; appointments etc. on time because they don't attach enough importance to being on time and as a consequence show disregard and a lack of respect for their colleagues and also a lack of professionalism. Being punctual therefore is not a matter of personal choice but a matter of whether you adhere to high work standards and professionalism.

The simple rule is to be punctual. If on an exceptional basis you can't attend a planned meeting on time then you should phone ahead prior to the meeting time and advise your colleagues of it. At that stage a decision can be taken to start the meeting without you or postpone to another time.

The bottom line is to be punctual and to respect your own and other people's time

### ACTION ITEMS

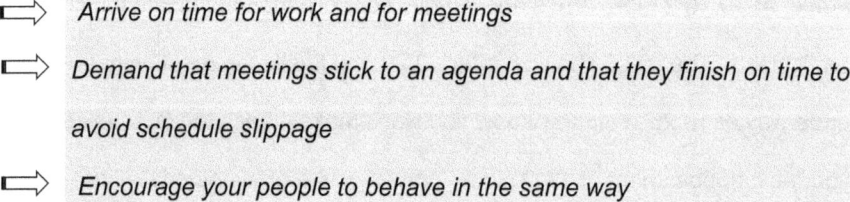

➡ Arrive on time for work and for meetings

➡ Demand that meetings stick to an agenda and that they finish on time to avoid schedule slippage

➡ Encourage your people to behave in the same way

*You Can Do Better!*

### 3.1.4 *Meet Commitments*

This is a central facet of your behaviour as an effective individual and manager. Whatever you commit to doing you ensure it is done and is delivered on time. The key pre-requisite in all of this is that you will make sensible judgements of your capabilities, capacity, time and efforts involved, and of other priorities and commitments before you make any new commitment. You understand completely that any promise you make you must deliver on as otherwise you will disappoint the target audience/higher management. If you fail to make commitments more than once, then apart from frustrating higher management you do significant harm to your trustworthiness and your reputation. This in turn can be career-limiting as higher management will delegate important work, priority projects etc. to those individuals and managers they can trust to deliver on their commitments.

### ACTION ITEMS

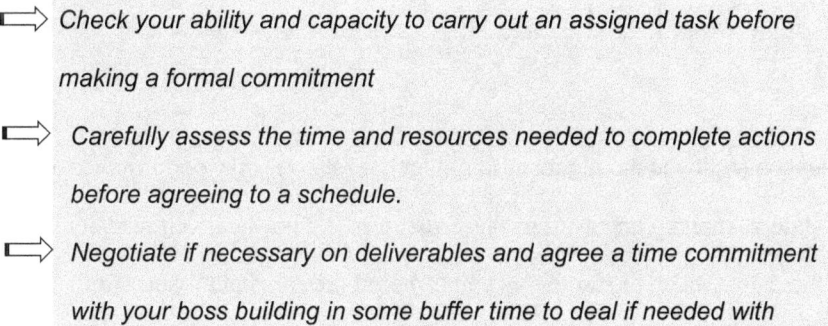

⇨ *Check your ability and capacity to carry out an assigned task before making a formal commitment*

⇨ *Carefully assess the time and resources needed to complete actions before agreeing to a schedule.*

⇨ *Negotiate if necessary on deliverables and agree a time commitment with your boss building in some buffer time to deal if needed with unforeseen problems. Push back if you feel strongly that it can't be done in the time proposed - you would only disappoint people otherwise.*

➪ *Keep higher management informed of progress and let them know as early as possible if some rescheduling is required.*

### 3.1.5 *Set stretching goals and targets for yourself and your people*

This idea comes under the realms of excellence and the notion that you get what you ask for. The basic idea is that if you ask for a little effort you probably will get a little. If on the other hand you ask for a lot you may well get a lot back or if not at least considerably more than if you had asked for a little. Shown graphically as follows;

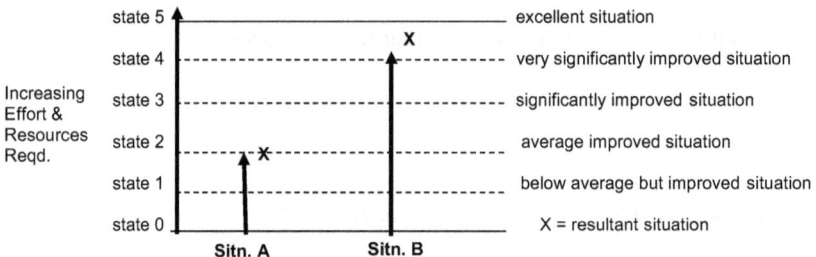

Situation (A) If you set a goal or target for the relatively low performance level of state 2 it can be achieved easily. Situation (B) If however you set your target at the outset much higher to say somewhere between state 4 and 5 and maybe you don't quite get there but get close to state 4.

42

# You Can Do Better!

Situation B is obviously preferable for a number of reasons…..

………….. you have achieved significantly more

…………. greater satisfaction for you/your people as a result

…………. it is highly probable that you/your people would be significantly challenged under situation B. Apart from the spur that a challenging experience provides it is also an excellent way of learning, growth and development for you and your people.

One important rider needs to be noted about goal setting at this point. It is important not to "over egg the pudding" and set the goal bar too high. If you do, all that will happen is that failure will result and people will become disillusioned and cynical despite their best efforts to achieve an impossible goal. Balance and good judgement is therefore needed to ensure target goals are achievable as well as being stretching.

## ACTION ITEMS

⇨ *Set goals that are doable, realistic and have a high degree of probability of successful completion*

⇨ *For some goals, at whatever level you judge the goal could be reasonably expected to be done, add an extra 15% - 20% stretch in some quantified target.*

⇨ *Along with the body of a stretch goal being achieved reward for the degree of stretch achieved in the goal results*

⇨ *Understand and communicate that the challenge of running with a stretching goal is to see how much of the "stretch" you/your people are able to achieve. It is decidedly not failure not to fully achieve the goal.*

### 3.1.6 *Work hard to eliminate shoddy work and poor work practices*

Being an effective manager who works to high standards you do not tolerate poor work performance or poor work practices. You directly confront situations of poor work performance and act swiftly to eliminate them.

Some practical examples of activities for you as a manager in this area are as follows;

- Return of poorly executed reports/memos etc. to their authors for timely correction
- Provide feedback on poorly prepared, poorly delivered presentations to presenters (generally in private)
- Insist on work punctuality
- Challenge the need for lengthy meetings, presentations etc.
- Demand a customer service ethic from all your staff with all internal and external parties
- Reset work standards and practices, which are identified as sub-standard.

There is one rider in all this of course. That is that you get the balance right and do not alienate people or get overly fussy and obsessive and essentially

44

you understand to deal with and correct the important sub-standard issues and ignore the trivial remainder.

**ACTION ITEMS**

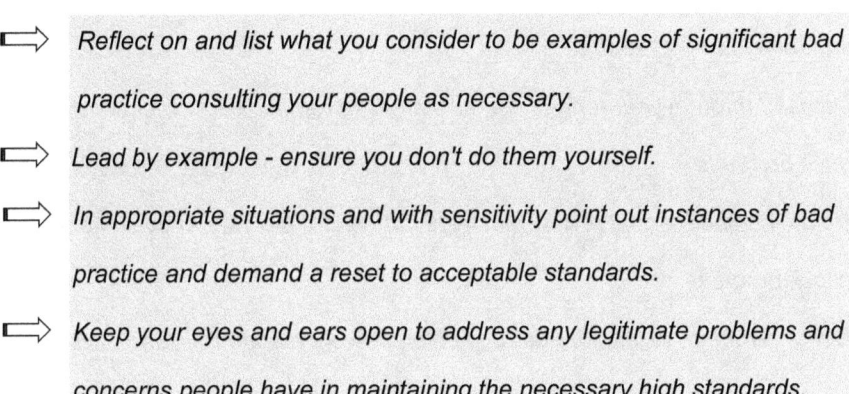

➡ *Reflect on and list what you consider to be examples of significant bad practice consulting your people as necessary.*

➡ *Lead by example - ensure you don't do them yourself.*

➡ *In appropriate situations and with sensitivity point out instances of bad practice and demand a reset to acceptable standards.*

➡ *Keep your eyes and ears open to address any legitimate problems and concerns people have in maintaining the necessary high standards.*

## 3.2 OPERATE BY "RESULTS THROUGH PEOPLE" PHILOSOPHY

meaning.............**YOU.....**

*Delegate responsibility readily and effectively*

*Drive communication, rapport building and work progress through regular 1-to-1 meetings with all reports*

*Demand through your reports that all staff have regular 1-to-1 meetings to drive progress*

*Hold a number of goal review meetings throughout the year to evaluate and check progress*

*Develop reports to take greater and different work responsibilities*

*Use personal authority minimally*

*Encourage measured risk taking by reports and focus on learning rather than on mistakes made*

*Hold a number of performance reviews with your reports throughout the year*

*Actively identify and encourage reports on employee development actions*

**Break-Out 3.2 OPERATE BY "RESULTS THROUGH PEOPLE"**

**PHILOSOPHY**

### 3.2.1 *Delegate responsibility readily and effectively*

The 1st law of management it is said is to delegate. It is a very important

quality for you, the effective manager to have particularly in these "time poor" times with potential for overload from e-mails, meetings, client interaction, staff

issues etc. Delegation of tasks and responsibilities to lower staff is a vital

activity for a number of reasons;

a) work should always be pushed down to the most appropriate staff levels

for completion for organisation efficiency reasons

b) delegating responsibility and appropriate work is an excellent staff

motivational and development exercise

c) it frees up managers to carry out more strategic, longer term actions

which are essential for the future of the business

d) it promotes organisational efficiency and increases organisational

capabilities, important traits to develop in an economically challenging

environment

By delegating appropriate work and responsibilities to your staff, you are being

more effective and there can be a certain payback in staff development and

greater engagement with the organisation.

A key issue of course is that the amount and level of delegated work is

appropriate and that the person is competent and trained to do the work.

As an effective manager you realise that you need to let go and freely delegate

work responsibilities to your staff as the occasion demands.

Delegation aids development, it frees up the organisation and increases the

organisation's responsiveness by spreading knowledge and aptitude across

the organisation. For managers who may be reluctant to delegate it is worth

*You Can Do Better!*

noting that if they persist in this behaviour, rather than becoming indispensable to the organisation (as they might think) they become isolated as the organisation moves on and new business and responsibilities are given to the more effective and higher achieving managers who freely delegate to their staff.

**ACTION ITEMS**

➡ *List activities and action plans you are currently working on and answer honestly the following 2 questions for each activity;*

*Is this the best and most effective use of your time?*

*Could someone else do all or part of the activity?*

*Assuming that you have identified activities or part activities that could be done as effectively by your reports then delegate the activity to them with clear instructions and a date for follow up.*

➡ *In your absence appoint by rote your various reports to take responsibility and coordinate selected duties you normally perform. Ensure that they are fully and clearly informed of what is required of them to complete the duties and that they are comfortable with doing them. On your return get feedback on how they got on and plan to repeat the exercise at suitable later dates.*

### 3.2.2 *Drive communication, rapport building and work progress through regular 1-to-1 meetings with your reports*

As an effective manager you understand at the outset that you need to establish and build rapport with all your staff reports. The best way to do this is to hold 1-to-1 meetings with each individual report. Individual meetings allow for individual attention where issues, problems and challenges can be discussed, debated and resolved openly which is not possible in the group situation. Also, needed feedback in both directions can be given which ultimately builds rapport. The 1-to-1 meeting is an excellent progress monitor for you as the manager as you can clearly gauge with your reportee, work in progress, and adherence to schedules, future work plans and action plans to address identified project deficiencies.

The agenda for the meeting is pre-set by you and should encompass all key current priorities (probably no more than 8) and communicated in advance. Separately the reportee apart from obviously updating his progress against priorities should bring his own agenda of items he wants to bring to discuss with you. The meeting itself generally follows the pattern of clearing your items first and then the reportee's. Routine items, news etc. should be left to the end of the meeting once all business issues have been discussed.

Durations of meetings can vary but may be typically 1 hour and should not surpass 1.5 hours. The frequency of the meetings will vary with the level of

49

your management responsibility and the number and level of your reportees. For lower level managers, weekly 1-to-1 meetings with his reports can be appropriate. For higher-level managers once every 2 to 3 weeks is probably more appropriate. Co-location can sometimes be a problem and hence 1-to-1 telephone meetings with pre-set and pre – emailed agendas can be managed. However telephone meetings are not as effective due to the lack of the obvious face-to-face communication.

## ACTION *ITEMS*

⇨ *Schedule 1-to-1 meetings with your reports at least monthly*

⇨ *Set up a simple agenda with no more than 8 items, communicate it to your reports  and have them do the same*

⇨ *Review 1-to-1 meeting effectiveness e.g. both parties come prepared to the meeting with 'homework' done, all main items covered in a business - like fashion, open  discussion on issues and concerns and 2 way feedback happening. Success is gauged by the fact that both parties see benefit and progress in holding the 1-to-1 meetings.*

### 3.2.3 *Demand through your reports that all staff have regular 1-to-1 meetings with all reports*

1-to-1 meetings if conducted properly in an open and sharing fashion are an excellent forum of 2-way communication, an excellent progress monitor and a

*You Can Do Better!*

great way to have a feel of the organisation's pulse. Therefore, as an effective manager you will do all in your power to encourage and when necessary demand the regular practice of 1-to-1 meetings between managers and reports at all levels.

Employees really appreciate it when proper efforts are made to sit down with them and discuss what's going on. It increases the flow of information downwards and upwards, and reduces the risk of nasty "surprises" being landed on managers' desks. 1-to-1 meetings improve general communications and morale (i.e. "I know I'm being listened to") and also reduce the need for informal ad hoc "head-in-the-door" discussions on important issues. It can also obviate the need for the office grapevine where rumours (often untrue) and scare mongering can thrive.

## ACTION ITEMS

⇒ *This comes from the success of your own 1-to-1 meetings with your reports. Set the expectation with your reports that they conduct formal progress reviews with their own staff the exact format and timing of which they can decide on between themselves.*

⇒ *Follow up periodically, perhaps every 2 months and check that formal meetings are happening at the required staff levels and within reasonable time intervals.*

### 3.2.4 *Hold a number of goal review meetings throughout the year to evaluate and check progress*

It is important of course to hold group meetings as well as individual 1-to-1 meetings throughout the year. Holding goal review meetings perhaps as often as one per quarter has distinct advantages;

- it holds people accountable to achieve progress - who wants to stand up and say they've achieved nothing!

- it updates everyone and creates a broad understanding of progress against goals

- it can act as a spur where deficiencies and gaps in performance are noted, to close them for the next period.

- it is a good general communications tool giving managers a forum for setting/resetting priorities going forward and also staff can air their views on the challenges and opportunities that lay ahead.

The precise running of a goal review meeting is open to individual management style but it goes without saying that the meeting should be business-like and not overly long and should be an interesting and informative exercise for those attending. It can also be a developmental exercise for e.g. new managers who are required to prepare and report against their section progress as part of the meeting.

### *You Can Do Better!*

The meeting should also be an open forum where opinions can be expressed about problems encountered/progress made and the general condition of the business.

Care needs to be taken as in all group meetings to ensure balanced participation, good time management and avoidance of getting off the point or into too much detail. The outcome of a good goal review meeting is that everyone can see and understand goal progress made and what future actions and priorities are need to be addressed to maintain momentum on progress.

**ACTION ITEMS**

➡ *Hold meetings perhaps once per quarter and issue a short agenda prior to the meeting. Allow short presentations only reflecting key goal performance and summary data only to maximise the opportunity for group discussion.*

➡ *As an alternate get the reports to set up the goal meeting and to report on the goal performance metrics themselves to increase their level of involvement*

➡ *Ensure that the objectives of the goal review process are clear, i.e.*

- *performance good and bad is discussed equally*
- *issues and concerns are openly discussed*
- *broad performance improvement ideas are discussed and agreed*
- *some discussion is also allowed on general issues affecting staff*

### 3.2.5 *Develop reports to take greater and different work responsibilities*

One of the often-quoted standard duties for you as a manager is that of developing your reports. Why would this be so? An obvious answer is that if you succeed in developing your reports then they can do and achieve more and hence make a greater on-going contribution to the organisation. Also it is important for succession planning reasons. While ultimate responsibility for personal development must remain with the individual, you as the manager have responsibility to be proactive in your report's development. You can approach this in a number of ways but certainly you will sit down with the report, discuss and document potential development areas (this may be as part of the performance appraisal process).

Also you may link with HR and your peer managers to identify what appropriate development work could be done either within your own function or within the wider business group function. Separately you may decide to delegate some of your work to your reports as a learning and development exercise, which can also give them a better appreciation for some of the broader issues being faced in the business. Another development assignment could be with the introduction of new management systems. In this case you could nominate your report to take responsibility for the introduction and smooth implementation of the new system on behalf of your department.

*You Can Do Better!*

The bottom line is that there should be 2 - way payback in this process, i.e. the business gets additional work done and the reports get some development and experience of taking on and working in broader roles.

**ACTION ITEMS**

⇨ *As part of the individual goal review/performance review process, discuss and agree with each report what's suitable and what may be possible. Agree outline action plans.*

⇨ *Involve HR and agree broad development actions and timelines with each report to follow up*

⇨ *If possible and practicable delegate some of your own responsibilities to your reports.*

⇨ *Periodically survey other departments/other parts of the business and actively follow up when suitable potential development assignments, new project work etc. is identified.*

### 3.2.6 *Use personal authority minimally*

As an effective manager you understand that the best way to get things done is to ask people in a polite and timely fashion. In cases where you do not have direct authority then you must use your influencing and persuasion skills and assuming that you have the respect of individuals then this tends to be a successful strategy. In almost all cases, barring emergencies it is better to suggest to people that they do something rather than tell them or worse to order them to do it.

As a manager you command respect mainly by the knowledge and experience you have, the contribution you make to the business, your (respectful) behaviour to others and to a lesser extent the position you hold within the company.

There can be instances where despite your best efforts work is not being done or standards being maintained. In such cases it is important that you stamp your authority on the situation and let people know clearly and directly what they need to do to close gaps and recover the situation.

Also, situations can arise where there is a difference of opinion and if you feel that you are on solid ground e.g. need for higher standards, then you need to direct the situation appropriately although such instances should be rare.

In conclusion as a manager you use your authority rarely and get things done through people by using appropriate asking/coaching/advising methods.

**ACTION ITEMS**

⇨ *Ask people politely to do what you need to get done. People respond better to requests and suggestions rather than orders.*

⇨ *Very occasionally you may come across a situation where peoples' behaviour is well below the normal standards required. On such occasions it is necessary and in fact you are obliged to use the authority of your position to quickly redress the situation, and let the people know clearly what standards of behaviour are required from them.*

### 3.2.7 Encourage measured risk taking by reports and focus on learning rather than on mistakes made

The person who never made a mistake does not learn much. The simple fact of the matter is that we learn from experience and some of that experience undoubtedly involves us jumping in and making mistakes. The key point is that we reflect on and learn from our mistakes and thus that we avoid making the same mistake again.

Seeking out new business opportunities, new management approaches etc. requires invention and innovation. It requires risk taking as we go into new territory that we have no experience of and hence can't know in advance.

As an effective manager you will encourage this risk taking in yourself and in your people. However the risk taking is not unbounded but contained e.g. use of pilot programmes to test the situation, use of seed capital with conditions and performance milestones, test and dummy runs, use of limited resources for trial periods etc. In this way your approach is measured by allowing the risk taking to happen but in a controlled way. You also understand that even when failure happens it is not the time to be disconsolate and for reprimands for your people but for learning to happen and discovery of what needs to happen differently in the future.

Nothing ventured, nothing gained. Risk taking is the leadership piece of management; it is the lifeblood of business strategy and building new business. Good managers like you know and understand this and are prepared to run with measured risk taking.

## ACTION ITEMS

⇨ *Encourage people to persevere when they are looking at setting up new methods of dealing with long held problems.*

⇨ *Task the group reporting to you to challenge at least 2 existing systems of administration and propose significant change or replacement.*

⇨ *Set a group goal to research and identify a new potential source of business and to set up a pilot scheme to exploit it.*

### 3.2.8 *Hold a number of performance reviews with your reports throughout the year*

The performance review process should consist of a few (perhaps two) mini reviews between yourself and your people during the year. In this way you can keep your people on track with their performance and when needed, steer them towards different behaviours if performance needs improvement. Also it is likely that goals will need to be added and/or changed during the year as a response to business changes.

The mini reviews are likely to cover a subset of people's goals and activities, which can then be simply updated at year-end by you for the annual performance review. Apart from the obvious benefit of providing on-going feedback, the use of mini reviews avoids major or nasty surprises for the employee at year-end if he is going to get some below par performance results in some areas. Ideally the performance review process should be a continuous one and not a one time a year event. Using a couple of mini reviews in this way helps to keep the necessary performance evaluation and feedback on track throughout the year.

One powerful way to help the review process along is for you to ask the employee to reflect on and list his personal achievements and disappointments throughout the year. When done honestly and well by the employee it contributes a lot to the review process as you as the manager get a greater understanding of the employee's position and standing.  Another approach is to ask the employee to rate himself on performance against each goal area and copy you prior to the review. This helps you to understand better the employee's expectations and the gaps between the employee's evaluation and your own evaluation of the employee.

**ACTION ITEMS**

⇨ *Schedule to have 2 review sessions with your reports within the year.*

*Hold a mini review at the mid-year interval which allows for a read-out*

*on how performance is generally going, and what performance issues*

*etc. the employee needs to tackle for the latter half of the year*

### 3.2.9 *Actively identify and encourage reports on employee development actions*

As an effective manager you understand very clearly that it's all about "results

through people" and that part of your job is to develop and grow people so that

they are more effective in themselves and can contribute more to the

organisation.

Hence you are very supportive of employee learning and development and

show real enthusiasm and encouragement when your people are

contemplating taking on training and development opportunities. You will take

time out and work with them to suggest and identify appropriate training areas.

You are likely to be active in or at least you will sponsor and be very supportive

of in house generated employee development programmes.

**ACTION ITEMS**

⇨ *As part of the review process twice per year (as suggested above) draft*

*what you feel are possible learning and development areas for each* report. Discuss the potential development areas with the report and get him to agree some concrete actions - perhaps no more than 3, to pursue throughout the year.

➡ Periodically, perhaps once per quarter review development plans with the report and what progress may have been made. Use the situation to encourage the report to continue with his development - it is for his own benefit after all.

➡ If necessary intervene if blockages to a report's development need to be removed or if other managers and/or e.g. HR personnel need to be communicated with to action development plans.

## 3.3 SELF-MANAGE

meaning............**YOU.....**

*Are an effective time manager*

*Continually set/reset priorities and are tenacious in follow through*

*Anticipate issues and problems with prompt follow-up to resolve them*

**Break-Out 3.3 SELF-MANAGE**

### 3.3.1 *Are an effective time manager*

As an effective individual you set your schedule around priorities and not the other way around. You understand the need to be disciplined, to put your head down throughout the day and make significant progress against your priorities. You manage your progress well, pacing yourself, doing more challenging work at your energy peak and leaving the more routine work for energy troughs. You are very focused on actions and do not allow distractions and interruptions interfere with your progress. You review your progress against set priorities a few times during the day to stay on target. You leave work when you are satisfied with the progress made on priorities and not because of what time it is. If you have a bad day due to unavoidable interruptions etc. you redouble your efforts the following day to get back on track. While you are much focused you are not time obsessive and actually you leave a proportion of your day free for unscheduled events. This allows you the necessary time for dealing with unplanned issues, having conversations with colleagues etc. and generally maintaining a human face along with a professional face.

The bottom line is that you are a doer and an achiever and you know that self-management and self-discipline is central in successfully meeting all your priorities.

**ACTION ITEMS**

➭ *Understand the important distinction between urgent and important items. Internalise it. Deal with the important items first. Urgent items second - unless they are true emergencies.*

➭ *Keep a time diary if necessary (in 1/2 hour slots) for one week to determine exactly where your time is going and how better it could be used. Note time wasters and avoid them.*

➭ *Use your diary to pace yourself and your workload throughout the day. Don't fill your diary thus always keeping time available for listening to people and dealing with the unexpected. Add time buffers to deal with unplanned over runs.*

### 3.3.2 *Continually set/reset priorities and are tenacious in follow through*

As an effective individual you are not happy to "wing it" every day and see what needs to be reacted to. You are proactive by nature and therefore you set your own priorities knowing that this gives you the best leverage and control of your job. Once priorities are set you go after each with a rigorous determination until they are completed to your satisfaction. Whatever you do not finish or get to you roll over to the next day or week as appropriate. Nothing falls through the cracks because you review progress carefully against action plans and close gaps in work as needed. You get significant satisfaction in completing tasks and closing priorities and this spurs you on to new ones. It is important to note that you regularly assess the situation versus the priorities you are currently working on. When you detect a change in the situation you quickly change, drop and/or add new priorities as appropriate.

As an individual and manager you work on anything between 1 - 6 priorities at any one time shuttling between each as progress is made. You are unlikely to have more than 6 priorities, as this would swamp your effectiveness. You also understand and make a clear distinction between priority items and routine items (e.g. administration) and you fit in routine items around priorities as time allows and not the other way round.

## ACTION ITEMS

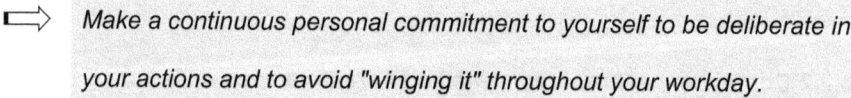

⇨ *Make a continuous personal commitment to yourself to be deliberate in your actions and to avoid "winging it" throughout your workday.*

⇨ *Plan your work diary before your working day (the same applies to week and month) and write down your priority actions.*

## You Can Do Better!

⟹ *Tenaciously progress your priority actions not allowing distractions to set you off course. Review and reset your priorities periodically as events dictate.*

⟹ *Fit routine work administration duties around when priorities are completed and/or your periods of low energy.*

### 3.3.3 Anticipate issues and problems with prompt follow-up to resolve them

This demonstrates your proactive nature as an effective individual and manager. You do not wait for things to deteriorate badly before you react to them. You remain alert and look for signals of change, get in early on changing situations to see what's going on and are quick to formulate a response and address the underlying problem issues. You then stay with the issues until you are happy that they are resolved. Your primary focus is to quickly fix issues as they arise, and the exact origin of the problems, who was involved etc., is of lesser importance to you.

### ACTION ITEMS

⟹ *Every so often lift your head up, take a break for 5 – 10 minutes taking a walk around and observe and assess what is happening and what people are doing/not doing.*

## *You Can Do Better!*

⇨ *On important/long action items hold regular review meetings to track progress against schedule and commitments.*

⇨ *Hold some time back to periodically challenge current action plans. Are they still suitable and do they fit appropriately with current events and the environment?*

⇨ *Be quick to reset thinking and action plans in the light of significantly changing events and environment.*

**Module 4**  | **Self-Management Ideas**

**3 self-management** ideas are discussed here and hopefully will give the reader pause for thought. With respect to clarity of thought everyone in his or her mind's eye can think of the nutty professor. He may be a genius but is dressed and groomed badly, is wildly scattered of thought and haphazard and ineffective in doing normal things. In the business situation we are all liable to the 'nutty professor' syndrome on occasion, especially when much is happening and many issues are clamouring for our attention. Everything seems to need attention but what's important to attend to? Time then, for some clear thinking!

A key point with the concept of contribution is that you have an accurate and realistic assessment of both your own contribution and of those you may report to you in your business. It is in effect the bottom line in terms of all your commitment and effort. The size of your contribution can say a good deal about your overall effectiveness although other factors can come into play such as your precise role and its connection to the core of the business. It is also important to recognise that the contribution you make will change over your career. As long as it is steady or increasing it is probably OK. However if your contribution is decreasing especially over a significant period, then it is time to ask questions and find out what you can do about it. The piece on learning

curves I think is self-explanatory.


## 4.1 Clarity of Thought

Can you see the wood from the trees? Using electronic parlance can you filter

the signal from the noise? Can you sort the vital few from the trivial many?

Clarity of thought is both a discipline and an ability which allows you analyse,

filter and make sense of your environment and following from this to know what

needs your time and attention, and as important, what does not, thus avoiding

trivial pursuits.


It is the ability to be able to simultaneously delve into the detail and yet also

take a broader view (readily switching between the two) so that you can form

an accurate picture of what's going on and hence figure out what you need to

do. It requires you to switch from the particular (the event) to the general (is

this a specific trend?) and switch back again.


It is an ability to distil, to summarise and accurately conclude on your

environment and its interactions and determine what's important, what needs

attention and what needs to be done. It gives you the plan or balcony view on events and interactions within your business operations and the interactions between the various players and participants.

Can you ascend in your mental helicopter and can you see what's happening (and not happening) on the ground between the various players?

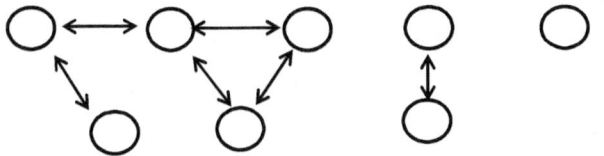

Clarity of thought requires you to take both a short and long term perspective on the business environment and from this form short and longer-term action items. It requires an uninterrupted focus on the business, and a calm reflection on business issues and events. With some clear thinking the situation can then be summarised, conclusions made and from there a purposeful and effective action agenda can be drawn up and progressed.

## 4.2 Your Contribution and Organisation Inventory

Suppose your business consists of 10 people and you are one of those people. Each person contributes something to the business and for the sake of clarity

## *You Can Do Better!*

let's say each contribution can be described by a circle the size of which

quantifies the contribution, i.e.,

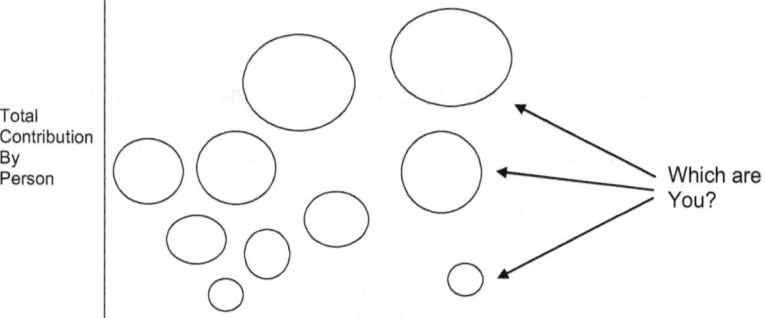

So what is the relative size of your circle and hence your contribution? Have

you been told or have you asked to find out? If you left the business, how much

of a loss would you be to the business?

The truth is that everyone contributes to different degrees to the business,

which is dependent on a number of key factors;

- o the person's position and role within the business

- o commitment, ability, experience and knowledge of the person in carrying

   out their role

- o the strength of the link between their current role and the critical success

   factors for the business

It is generally accepted that people's contribution can be categorised as;

A - Making consistent large on-going contributions to the business

B - Making consistent medium/average on-going contributions to the business

C - Making consistent small on-going contributions to the business

### *You Can Do Better!*

It is likely that the 'B' type are the biggest grouping within the business and are the "Steady Eddies" – very necessary people with steady but unlikely ever to be scintillating performance. 'A' type people are a smaller group who are the high potential people, i.e. contributing a lot at the level of their current roles and are likely to progress and advance further and make greater contributions as time goes on. 'C' type people are hopefully also a small group of people who make a small contribution for a variety of reasons; e.g.

➤ mismatch between their current roles and their abilities

➤ low engagement and hence low commitment to the organisation

➤ low competence and low ability to fulfil the role

➤ not adequately trained in the role

➤ low energy - people suffering from burnout

➤ external factors limiting their performance

Obviously both A and B type people are needed within the organisation. C type people need to be monitored, retrained, or redeployed into more suitable roles consistent with their ability and to increase their commitment and engagement with the organisation. Otherwise, they need to be removed from the business. Organisation inventory therefore is an exercise generally carried out at business management level where people are evaluated as to their contribution level to the organisation (A, B or C) and then matched to a series of potential development and or promotional moves across the organisation of the business. These moves are planned into the future both as part of the individual's career development but also as part of organisation strengthening and development. Varied time scales for people development moves are used depending on the readiness of the individuals as well as that of the organisation amongst other factors.

Typical time scales used could be;

Ready Now: Within 1 Year;  1 - 3 Years and Greater than 3 years

One alternate option of course for the organisation is that if no one can be identified within the organisation to fill a particular role then external candidates can be pursued. Recruitment of external people can also be a positive for the business in terms of bringing in fresh thinking and different skills to the business and perhaps also shaking up a staid culture within the business.

## 4.3 Learning Curves and Career Progression

Your career over time consists of a series of learning curves. What is a learning curve?

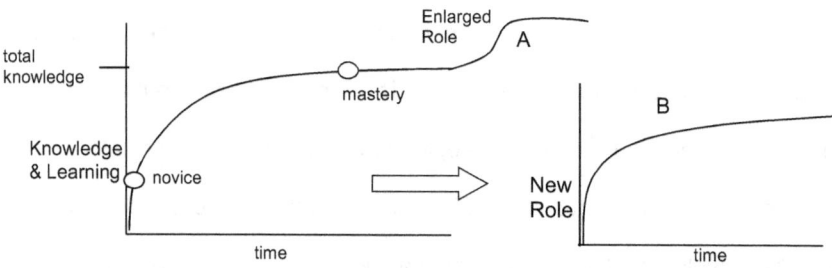

## *You Can Do Better!*

As the curve shows when you begin a new role your knowledge is obviously very limited and hence you start off as a novice. The development curve is steep and hence your rate of learning and personal growth in a short space of time rises sharply until you reach a shoulder at which point in time you will have gained a significant amount of knowledge and experience of the role and hence your development rate now rapidly reduces (heading towards an almost flat line) as you progress towards role mastery.

You will never know everything about the role but it is likely that after a number of years you will have mastered the role in large measure. At this point on the curve learning and personal growth and development is very limited and the issue becomes can you enlarge your role and hence extend your ultimate learning curve as shown in situation A or as in situation B switch to a new role and hence move to a totally new learning curve?

Key points about learning curves are;

I. if you are on an upward slope this is generally a good thing as it is likely that you are engaged with the organisation and are learning and developing significantly.

II. if you are on the flatter part of the curve then you either have already achieved or are close to role mastery. If you have been on the flat part of the curve for some time, say a couple of years, then what does this say? It means you are not developing (at least significantly) and you are essentially doing the same job and making the same contribution year on year. Being "flat lined' in your learning - career progression is not necessarily a bad thing at least for a while. Remaining in the same role for a certain amount of time can consolidate your learning and development and build your self-assurance and self-confidence in your role.

III. However at some point in time it is advisable to look for new roles and further growth and development opportunities. Otherwise you need to make the choice yourself of arriving at your on-going competence level and as such at the 'ceiling of your career'. For some people this is an important and welcome milestone, i.e. they have fulfilled their ambition and are generally happy to stay at the role level that they are at.

So it begs the questions - where are you on your career and development curve, are you happy with your position on the curve and if not, what are you doing about it to grow further?

**Module 5**  |  **Practical Thinking Ideas**

**This is** all about coming from different angles and perspectives to increase your flexibility in thinking your way through and possibly on occasion, out of situations. The ultimate response you give in any situation is as a direct result of the quality of your thought process on your position. The greater the scope you have in your thinking will allow you to have a greater range of possible responses in any given situation. *A central point here is that it's not so much what happens to you that's important but rather the response you choose to give in the situation* - *choose being the operative word here.* Using a number of thinking ideas is, if you like, thinking with more than one head.

The use of 3rd party thinking helps to remove immediate emotional impulses and the distractions they cause, giving you greater capacity to respond clearly and well in difficult situations.

Taking polar opposite views can also help with your thinking, i.e. it stops you running with the first half baked idea you thought of (the rush to action) without identifying and giving due consideration to the merits of other options.

Finally, being conscious of what approach you are using and where your focus is on (task, individual or group) at any one point in time in a given situation is an important part of self-awareness of your own behaviour. The issue here is that you are self-aware, deliberate and conscious of the approach you're using and that it is appropriate and fits with the situation in hand.

## 5.1 The Broader View

A common failing that people can have is that they have a narrow view and short-term focus on their role within the organisation. They recognise only their own area and responsibility and are only interested generally in their own area and in some instances can become proprietorial and territorial about their area of responsibility.

Development though, demands a broader view needs to be taken. This means to take an interest in activities and issues happening outside your own area of the business. By doing so, this broadens the person's understanding of how the wider business operates a vital attribute to have if one is to move on to other roles and areas within the business.

Another key issue that the broader view helps with is that of collaboration. With ever increasing business pressures and the need to get maximum use of existing resources senior management recognise the need to maximise collaboration and identify with those individuals and managers who show abilities to work in tandem with their counterparts in other areas of the business sharing information, expertise and resources thus providing a greater contribution and value add to the business as a whole.

As a manager's career progresses his role necessarily becomes larger and he can find himself dealing with a range of priorities some of which may be conflicting. It is his ability to take the broader view and a longer-term focus that helps him to understand the impact and contribution of each priority and ultimately guides him to maintain an effective balance between priorities.

## 5.2 Thinking like your Boss

Your boss or manager has to deal with a broader range of responsibilities and issues. He has numerous priorities, staff with a variety of problems to deal with, various constraints and limited resources and he has budget and cost control targets to achieve.

If you can take time to understand your manager's role and responsibilities you will be in a better position to anticipate what is needed from you and to both meet and manage the expectations of your manager. Hence, this in itself will increase your effectiveness. Also it impresses on your manager that you are on top of your role and can deliver required results when expected and needed.

If you are ever to become the boss yourself the first step might be to try and put yourself in his shoes and build understanding of his role. Expanding on this thought, for those who have significant ambition to rise within the business it is an important asset to take some time out to develop a good understanding of the nature of higher management roles and responsibilities. A good point to start with is to ask your manager to share with you his thinking and understanding of his role. With increased awareness and understanding of higher roles you increase your potential for developing further in the future organisation. Can you step up to your boss's level and think like your boss?

## 5.3 Taking 3rd Party Views

This is a powerful thinking method in maintaining objectivity even though you may in the "thick of the action". Simply put, it is to imagine yourself to be a third party observer of what is happening and therefore from a thought process viewpoint taking a step back from the action and calmly observing what is happening. The 3rd party observer is interested in what is happening but is not emotionally invested in the situation and hence can take an objective, calm and dispassionate view of the events and issues which are unfolding. To use a metaphor it is like having a little man perched on your shoulder who is observing 1st, commenting on what's going on and then giving options as to what your response should be in the situation.

The value of this approach to switch from 1st person to 3rd person thinking is that it removes the manager from the immediate situation This mental removal allows him to calm down, observe the situation and himself, take a more objective viewpoint thus enabling him to develop the most appropriate and effective response to the situation he finds himself having to manage. In summary, when caught up in a difficult situation think as if you are an outsider (e.g. a United Nations observer) who has as they say "no axe to grind" and hence it is likely that such 3rd party thinking will result in better and more clear thinking by you and ultimately in a better response to the situation in hand.

## 5.4 Janusian Thinking

Janusian thinking refers to the ability to take diametrically opposed views to an issue at the same time and after thinking about and analysing both views being able to see the merits and potential shortcomings of both views. By taking the initial effort and time to identify and understand both sides of the argument as it were, the individual is better equipped and better positioned to tackle the issue. Also of course, he is better prepared if and when someone taking the opposite view to his preferred one confronts him -, i.e. he has already seen the other side and can have some empathy with it.

Another simple analogy is that of the debating process. Team A is assigned to argue in favour of e.g. a particular course of action and charged with identifying key benefits and advantages associated with it. Team B is assigned to refute the particular course of action by identifying key outcome losses and disadvantages of the particular action and arguing against it. The resultant debate and discussion if properly handled can be very revealing as new views come to light on both sides giving greater clarity and balance to the issues and to the particular course of action which might be preferred.

A subsidiary method is to take the contrarian view, i.e. play the Devil's advocate against whatever is proposed and sponsored by the majority view, i.e. the contrarian takes the minority view and "goes against the head" so to speak. Of course it is not necessarily that the contrarian view is correct but because it challenges the majority held view (sometimes called 'groupthink') it can lead to reconsideration and additional debate. This can bring more clarity and weight to the pros' and cons' of an issue increasing the chance of a more effective solution being found in the end.

## 5.5 The 3 Circles Leadership Model

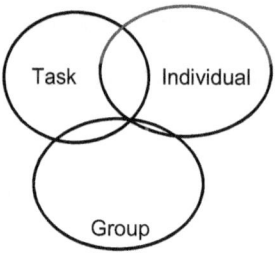

As a manager it is important to understand where your focus of attention is at any point in time and to ensure your attention is in the right place. Managers with a task focus are concentrating on actually doing and achieving whatever tasks and goals are set out. Managers with an individual focus are more concerned with the individuals they are responsible for and spend considerable time with them at 1-to-1 meetings.

Managers with a group focus clearly concentrate not on the task in hand or the individuals but on the group of people they are responsible for as a whole. Their approach to the job is to involve the whole group or work team in pursuing the work and output of the unit.

Which approach and focus is right? The answer is that all three approaches are correct and the precise one used at any one time will vary with the circumstances and the context of the situation.

For example, in an emergency or an urgent situation the manager would clearly be in task mode to overcome the particular difficulty. The task focus is also appropriate if pressing results are needed and set goals are behind schedule. In an on-going normal management situation the 1-to-1 individual approach is probably the most appropriate. This is because communications can be at their most effective in the 1-to-1 situation between the manager and his individual reportees. Expectations and needs can be clearly expressed on both sides and progress against goals and task schedules can be readily monitored. It is also the best forum for resolving and clarifying issues and problems and removing obstacles to progress.

# *You Can Do Better!*

The group or team approach can be best suited when a project or body of work is needed to be done requiring a variety of skills and where individuals on their own could not hope to complete the work needed. The group approach can bring advantages such as team building and bonding towards a common purpose and goals, taking a unified approach and acting as a unit. Also by effectively combining skills and knowledge greater work achievement is possible. Care needs to be taken to ensure there is balanced participation in groups and that potential group domination by individuals, politicking etc. is carefully managed. The manager may also use the group focus approach when he detects lack of cohesion and overly individualistic attitudes and behaviour. In such cases he uses the group approach to push for collaboration between individuals and a more unified response from the group.

Group work can take time to set up and also requires on-going management and hence at the outset only appropriate work should be assigned to groups, i.e. work which can be done effectively by individuals should be done first. In certain situations it is likely that the boundaries between each focus approach will overlap and hence the manager may be using 2 approaches at once, the exact 2 used depending on the circumstances and context of the situation and people involved.

In summary the 1-to-1 individual focus approach is likely to be the starting point for most management situations but switching to the task and group approach will also be required as the occasion demands. So, what approach are you using? Is it effective and are you capable of switching focus appropriately as undoubtedly will be demanded of you as your situation changes?

**Module 6**   | **Key Leadership Ideas In Action** |

**The routine** (core business) needs to be maintained and prolonged as efficiently as possible. However, without development, the routine will gradually disappear. Why? Because the core business, left unchanged, will diminish over time as the environment changes.

Hence the notion of the duality of maintenance and development, i.e. you need both to survive. Development means changing, adding to and/or replacing the existing business with a new type of business. It requires exploring new territory and invention and innovation of new business streams and methods. It requires people who know they don't know because they are prospectors and explorers of new business territory, and yet they are prepared to go forward and take the necessary risks. In short, they are business leaders

## 6.1 Maintenance and Development

Maintenance is the management piece and development is the leadership piece. Maintenance is about controlling and prolonging the routine e.g. maintaining customer service at certain levels, maintaining invoicing and reporting systems etc.

Maintenance is about doing the thing right and retaining the status quo, a vital activity up to a point. However, you must also have development, which is about doing the right thing. To illustrate the point consider the difference between company A working on improving rewind speeds of their VCR recorder product versus company B working on their new Blu Ray DVD recorder product. Company B is doing the right thing, i.e. development, whereas Company A - maintenance is doing the thing right - unfortunately not the appropriate thing any longer.

Another analogy that can be used is the difference between incremental (continuous) improvement and step change (one time large change) improvement. Both are important; incremental / continuous improvement normally associated with maintenance activities, i.e. gradually improving existing conditions. Step change improvement on the other hand is associated with development activities, i.e. significant changing and/or introducing new conditions.

Maintenance and development activities are both important with maintenance being an on-going *evolutionary* activity, (i.e. continuous incremental improvement) and development being a periodic *revolutionary* activity as business conditions either allow or demand, i.e. where fundamental operational changes or new business management systems are needed.

## 6.2 Scriptwriting

The analogy being used here is of the Hollywood film scriptwriter. To make a film successfully you need a script and a scriptwriter. In business, to have a successful business you need somebody writing a script or strategy that is suitable and fits with the business environment. Following on then, how do you develop abilities to be a scriptwriter? Clearly you must have a deep understanding of at least some of a number of your business elements e.g.

- the basic business model, what is adding value, what range of benefits you can give to customers
- the current business environment, the competition, current and likely future changes in the environment
- current profit margins, current costs and financial projections
- nature of the operations of the business and the critical success factors in maintaining the operations
- key staff and employee issues
- roles of key systems and functions employed, critical to maintenance of the business

Of course, it is unlikely that someone could have a deep knowledge and understanding of all the business elements. What is important though is that scripts are written and strategies are developed for the business. Clearly therefore, there are likely to be several scriptwriters in the business who are jointly making strategy and developing the business. Are you a scriptwriter? What would it take to become one? This leads onto the next area of leadership, i.e. strategy and business development.

## 6.3 Strategy and business development

Strategy is concerned with development rather than (routine) maintenance activities. It is about working from 1st principles and taking a new approach to the business. It is about applying the deep knowledge and understanding gained of the business model, the specific value-adds and the business environment, to develop a business plan. *Having a successful strategy means being in tune with the external environment.* The business plan or strategy is thus your best response to the current and future predicted business environment and it will specify at least broad action plans you intend to take to further your business in the future. Action plans can be of an external and internal nature, i.e.

> external - customer development, business prospecting etc.
> internal - introducing better business management and operational practices and systems, cost reduction projects etc.

The strategy in action is likely to be a longer-term plan perhaps taking from anywhere between 1 - 3 years to implement. It also needs to be a work in progress plan i.e. it can be revised and developed on the run based on existing and changing business conditions. It goes without saying that the strategy

*You Can Do Better!*

needs full and proactive support of senior management to implement and that

task and event schedules and performance milestones need to be clearly

mapped out.


**Business Development:**

Key issues for any business development plans are;

(a) Is the existing business model working?

(b) What are the trends in the key metrics sales revenues, sales margins,
and service/product costs?

(c) Market size/growth/contraction

(d) Competitor activities

(e) Where are you in the business life cycle? i.e. growth - maturity –
stagnation – decline

(f) Are there any growth areas within your existing business to prospect?
- if so what are they and how are you going to exploit them?

(g) If the existing business has matured what new business areas can
you identify that have opportunities?

(h) What business pilots can you run and what resources do you need to
prospect for new business areas?

(i) Are there aspects of your existing business areas you need to exit and
therefore provide freed up resources in more promising business
areas?

*You Can Do Better!*

(j) Within your organisation who are your identified business prospectors and what specific goals do they have on developing new and existing businesses?

(k) What practical strategies can you use to link with potential new clients to the point that they are ready and willing to do business with you e.g. referrals, business pilots, service trials, small contracts etc.

*You Can Do Better!*

## Module 3 | Behaviours of an Effective Individual and Manager |

### PART 2

**What follows** is the 2$^{nd}$ part of the effective individual's module with 4

behaviours

The behaviours described below can be prefaced by the word – **YOU**

## 3.4 ARE ACHIEVEMENT ORIENTED

meaning.............**YOU**.....

*Focus concentration on action planning, progress monitoring and goal*

*completion*

*Are single minded and determined in task completion*

**Break-Out 3.4 ARE ACHIEVEMENT ORIENTED**

**3.4.1** *Focus concentration on action planning, progress monitoring and*

*goal completion*

As a committed individual you are a doer and an achiever. You derive your

satisfaction from carefully setting up your task schedule and systematically

knocking off all planned activities until the overall goal is completed. A

metaphor, which can be used, is that of a highly paid professional hit man.

Once the contract is set and the money is handed over you know the "hit" or

job is going to be completed. There is no going back. Why? - Because of total commitment and professionalism. In the same way as an effective individual you have a deep professional pride and connection in what you do and once the project is set, you will use all your efforts, skills and experience in its progress to the project's ultimate completion. You identify closely with it and hence invest heavily of yourself (it's more than just a job) to ensure it gets done. It's a matter of professional pride and honour for you. Also, remember that your professionalism as an individual and manager becomes the standard of behaviour you want to see in your team of people.

## ACTION ITEMS

➡ *Carefully set out action plans to achieve your business goals on a daily/weekly/monthly basis.*

➡ *Get your head down, focus on the doing and progress will be the spur to continue.*

➡ *Tick off items as they are completed and reward yourself with mini breaks.*

### 3.4.2 *Are single minded and determined in task completion*

When you are working on a project you are like the proverbial dog with a bone. You will keep working on it and working on it and will not get distracted by external events unless relevant to the project. You thrive on making progress and task completion, which is a great source of work satisfaction to you. You do of course, retain an interest in other business issues but they are of secondary importance to you. Task and project completion comes first for you and you are resolute and unwavering in carrying this out. Also of course, as tasks are progressed you keep an eye on your people to ensure that healthy team dynamics are being maintained.

## ACTION ITEMS

⇨ *Commit yourself 100% to doing and achieving. Always remember that the smallest deed is greater than the biggest intention. So don't just sit there and intend. Do!*

⇨ *Every day before work's end review what you have actually done versus what you set out to do. 90%+ means a good day. Less than 90% means a bad day. Do the same at the end of the week and the end of the month. Don't sweat the bad days – just make sure you have many more good days!*

⇨ *Concentrate and focus and work hard for short time periods - perhaps 40 – 50 minutes. Take plenty of breaks in between to rest. When you are tired you can afford to give in to distractions or do some routine administration work as required. Pace yourself well throughout the day getting the most out of your high energy/high brainpower periods.*

## 3.5 ARE SELF-DEVELOPING

meaning.............**YOU**.....

*Encourage feedback on your own performance to identify development areas*

*Seek out appropriate self-development training for yourself and your staff*

*Are proactive in developing your career path*


**Break-Out  3.5 ARE SELF-DEVELOPING**

**3.5.1** *Encourage feedback on your own performance to identify development areas*

A precondition for this quality of course, is that not only do you need to be comfortable with receiving feedback (some of which is likely to paint you in an unfavourable light) but also you should positively seek it out! Who rushes out to find (some) bad news about themselves? The answer is that as an effective individual you have a realistic view of yourself; you know you have strengths and limitations. You also know that if you get objective feedback on your strengths and limitations that you can work further on them thus accelerating your development. You also know that feedback for you is useful as you can gauge personal progress and it can alert you to blind spots about aspects of your behaviour which you may need to change. You are confident enough and self-assured in your own abilities that you see feedback from others as an important method to better understand your position and what you need to do to further your development.

### *You Can Do Better!*

Interestingly, people working with you feel comfortable because they know they can discuss sensitive issues with you without you feeling that this is a personal attack on you or your authority. A key balancing point of course, is that you do not allow a "free for all" situation develop where anyone with perceived issues and/or grudges can lay them at your door.

The feedback you as an individual and as a manager work on needs to be genuine, given with an objective basis and from this position you understand and can agree that some reflection and change on your part may be required.

## ACTION ITEMS

⇨ *Reflect periodically on the quotation "If only you could see yourself as others see you"*

⇨ *Firstly get comfortable with the idea of soliciting feedback from others. Ease into the process by asking your spouse/partner, your close friends and/or a trusted colleague to give you feedback on your behaviour. An example would be ..... Your top 3 good points are, and 3 areas you are weak at/need to work on are.......*

⇨ *Extend the process over a period of time, as you get comfortable with it to include your boss/higher management, your peers and your reports.*

⇨ *Thank everyone on feedback received and especially for being candid with you. Encourage them to continue with the feedback when the opportunity arises. Reflect on the feedback and accept it. (at least to the extent that other people's perceptions of you are real to them and you need to do something to change yourself or to alter their perceptions)*

⇨ *Act on feedback by changing your behaviour or replacing redundant behaviours with more effective behaviours.*

### 3.5.2 Seek out appropriate self-development training for yourself and your staff

As an effective self-manager you do not wait for someone e.g. your boss, HR etc. to approach you and suggest training for you. You are proactive in this yourself, working either on your own initiative or with HR to identify potential training needs. Having identified training areas you will likely discuss them with your boss to clarify and get broad agreement on training and development priorities. You will then use this as a blueprint for action and will set up a broad schedule for completion over the following twelve months.

The training plan could encompass a range of development activities for yourself and your staff including;

   budgeting and financial planning

   customer service and marketing

   core management skills training - e.g. staff appraisal, time management, meetings management etc.

   computer skills and systems training

project management

in house training on new systems/programmes

management development e.g. taking up new/extra areas of

responsibility or taking up special projects

coaching skills

You clearly understand that your development is your own responsibility and therefore are proactive in ensuring your own training is completed and you are continually on the lookout for new training and development opportunities as your career progresses.

## ACTION ITEMS

⇨ *Be particularly interested in areas for your development as part of your performance review process. Your boss and/or HR should be able to help you identify targeted training and development areas for you.*

⇨ *Be proactive in completing all targeted and specific training programmes for yourself. This is after all for your benefit - not anyone else's. Your development should include on the job training by taking on enlarged roles, different roles, and special project work etc.*

⇨ *You are only as good as your team capability and hence you need to challenge your people to prioritise their development. Challenge them to be proactive in developing themselves by identifying training and development areas for themselves. Help them do this as part of the performance review process or separately at appropriate 1-to-1 meetings. Encourage your staff to sit down with HR to determine development possibilities. Remember finally that it is up to your staff individually to actively pursue and progress their own development. Your function is to initially prompt them and then coach them and guide them as needed.*

### 3.5.3 *Are proactive in developing your career path*

You understand that the only person responsible for your development is yourself. You equally know that you need to be proactive in developing your own career and not be passively reliant on your boss, higher management or the HR dept. that may or may not be interested.

You therefore periodically scan the business for career development opportunities, which may be appropriate for yourself and pursue them when a suitable opening arises. You do this with political tact using your boss and HR channels as a conduit to potential opportunities.

The springboard for advancement of course, is that you are very good and proficient at your existing job and have gained sufficient experience such that you can now move on. It is also helpful if a staff member replacement for your existing position can be readily found. It is vital too of course that higher management are in agreement, i.e. you are ready now and capable of moving on to a new position with development potential.

## *You Can Do Better!*

Examples of potential moves are;

- taking on enlarged roles with more responsibility

- taking lateral moves to increase personal versatility and flexibility

- taking on special management sponsored projects

- getting involved in intercompany task teams at higher management request

- overseas assignments if appropriate

- taking charge of implementing new management systems for the company

- linking activities and roles with other business divisions and functions

## ACTION ITEMS

⇨ *Develop a 5-year plan listing jobs/roles (maximum of 3) you believe you would both like and be capable of growing into over the time period.*

⇨ *List qualities and particular skills and expertise you believe you need to be successful in the roles. Identify what potential steps and interim roles you could take to progress towards the positions of interest.*

⇨ *Review and discuss your identified future potential roles with your boss and potential action plans. Agree concrete steps and broad time scales for action e.g. taking on enlarged roles with more responsibility, different roles to increase experience, which will help progress your development.*

## 3.6 ARE REFLECTIVE

meaning…………..**YOU**…..

*Are reflective on successes and failures and what to do differently*

*Converse with your trusted others on issues to broaden your understanding and to clarify your thoughts*

*Think through situations to determine possibilities before deciding on action*

*Suspend judgement; maintain flexibility in your thinking in complex/ambiguous situations*

### Break-Out 3.6 ARE REFLECTIVE

**3.6.1 *Are reflective on successes and failures and what to do differently***

As a self-manager you periodically take stock of what has worked for you and what has not worked. You will retain the behaviour which leads to good results and will try new approaches in cases in which your impact and effectiveness needs to improve.

### ACTION ITEMS

⟹ *Take a half hour "downtime" out at the end of the week to reflect on and answer in your own mind 2 basic questions*

    *1. What went well for me and why? (so that you can repeat it)*

    *2. What did not go well and how can I do better on this next week?*

## 3.6.2 *Converse with your trusted others on issues to broaden your understanding and to clarify your thoughts*

There is a philosophy which states; the way to know and clarify your thinking is to hold a conversation with another on the issues. A trusted other is likely to be a peer, your boss or another manager or even your spouse. The point is you can have an open conversation with the other person in confidence, who will listen to you and can give clarity to your expressed thoughts and on occasion give you feedback on perspective, on what's important and what can be ignored etc.

## ACTION ITEMS

⇨ *Perhaps once a month sit down with your trusted other - be it with your mentor, boss, trusted colleague etc. Discuss your understanding of the major events and business interactions that occurred, what you did and said and your overall conclusions and feelings of what you experienced.*

⇨ *Bounce your thoughts off the other person including your fears, concerns, and frustration as they relate to your conclusions of what's going on. This can significantly help you to clarify your own thoughts and stance on issues as well as help you to reset misconceptions.*

### 3.6.3 *Think through situations to determine possibilities before deciding on action*

The salient point here is that on important issues you take some time to consider your options and the choice of actions open to you before you act which gives you a better chance of being more successful.

**ACTION ITEMS**

⇨ *Get into the habit of checking yourself and pausing thus avoiding impulsive action. Check and consider carefully as best you can on what you propose to do and what options are open to you before launching into action.*

⇨ *Keep your action plans fluid and as flexible as possible so that you can readily change course without major difficulty when the need arises.*

### 3.6.4 *Suspend judgement; maintain flexibility in your thinking in complex/ambiguous situations*

In complex situations or situations that are continuing to evolve it is difficult if not impossible to predict the outcome. Hence it is most prudent to maintain flexibility in thinking and not to make any hard and fast judgements and decisions until the situation clarifies itself or at least that you are more confident about the probable outcome. In these situations, sitting on things, listening to your gut, sleeping on it are the more effective strategies.

*You Can Do Better!*

**ACTION ITEMS**

⇨ Remember the line, "Don't just do something, stand there!" In ambiguous or fast changing situations it can be best to delay action until the situation clarifies itself and the specific action needed becomes more apparent.

⇨ Ignore the rush to action in yourself or perhaps coming from your reports. Schedule your decision to action to give you enough time to think through unfolding events. Let tentative decisions simmer overnight and if they still taste right in the morning then go ahead and act on them.

## 3.7 ARE PERSONABLE WITH SOCIAL SKILLS

meaning…………..**YOU**…..

*Show genuine and active interest in people*

*Operate by relationship 1st, business 2nd rule*

*Engender positive working relationships with peers, superiors and reports*

*Make regular daily efforts to converse with people 1-to-1 and in groups*

*Are comfortable with ability to both lead and be part of teams*

*Show ability to develop teamwork and collaborative work ethic amongst work groups*

*Attune to local and organisational politics and become adept in successfully navigating through politically charged situations*

*Are an effective net worker, identify and collaborate with significant others*

### Break-Out 3.7 ARE PERSONABLE WITH SOCIAL SKILLS

#### 3.7.1 *Show genuine and active interest in people*

Acknowledge people, smile at them, and talk with them for a little while.

Act naturally with them - don't force it and for God's sake don't try to fake it.

#### ACTION ITEMS

⇨ *Develop a daily and/or weekly routine to mingle with your people*

⇨ *Briefly clear your mind and focus your total attention on the person you are speaking to and show an active interest in what they are saying.*

### 3.7.2 *Operate by relationship 1st, business 2nd rule*

Remember you are a human being first and that you have to make a living second.

**ACTION ITEMS**

⇨ *Always acknowledge and greet the person first in a friendly and respectful way. Then, discuss the business issues.*

### 3.7.3 *Engender positive working relationships with peers, superiors and reports*

Simply put, the individual and manager who makes the continuous effort to have genuine and positive working relationships with the people he deals with will be more influential and successful in the long run.

**ACTION ITEMS**

⇨ *Take the necessary time and effort to converse and in particular to listen to people. Be positive and supportive when you can .Be attentive to their interests and needs. Make it a routine to develop relationships and build rapport with them over time.*

*You Can Do Better!*

### 3.7.4 *Make regular daily efforts to converse with people 1-to-1 and in groups*

Time constraints apply of course but sometimes all that's needed is "hello, how are you today"?

**ACTION ITEMS**

⇨ *Even at your busiest it is always wise to take one minute of your time to say hello to people and genuinely acknowledge them.*

### 3.7.5 *Are comfortable with ability to both lead and be part of teams*

The effective individual and manager has a deep understanding of what effective teamwork entails, the need for balanced participation, the different roles required in teams, the need to subsume the individual persona for the good of the team, effective individual and team building traits and behaviours, the need for process review to ensure cohesive team working and the presence of team norms and rules to keep things on track, and to keep inappropriate and disruptive behaviours in check. With this understanding of what works in teams he is thus confident in leading teams and overcoming barriers and obstacles that are normally encountered as the team forms and develops over time, until such time that the team is effective and is performing as a unit.

When the manager is part of a team himself he ensures his contribution is positive and balanced, that he is an effective listener and quickly identifies and adopts the role best suited to his needs and to team needs. He uses his best efforts to ensure that team goals are progressed over individual goals and preferences. He collaborates well, avoids taking sides, and pushes for unified approaches and solutions. He identifies with the team and all team members and remains positive and friendly working through problems and issues, which are causing conflict. He encourages other team members in their efforts and directs himself and other members in performing the required concerted actions to achieve the overall goals of the team

## ACTION ITEMS

⇨ *There are many good textbooks on teamwork and teambuilding. Read some and reflect on the key points to ensure that you understand the essentials and the essence of good teamwork*

    *e.g. everyone in the team has a role and a voice*

    *balanced participation with no one trying to dominate or win*

    *A unified approach to action and problem solving*

    *Each member is helpful and supportive of each other*

    *There is a common purpose and people are action oriented*

    *There is healthy feedback between team members*

    *Good team process is important in achieving sustainable team results*

⇨ *Proactively volunteer to be both part of teams and to be a leader of teams (e.g. project coordinator). Reflect on experiences gained – what worked, and what did not. Encourage and act on feedback you receive*

*on your performance as both a team player and a team leader*

### 3.7.6 *Show ability to develop teamwork and collaborative work ethic amongst work groups*

While the manager in the main will look for a strong individual contribution from everyone (as part of the 1-to-1 meeting process) he insists also that on-going occasions demand that those working in the same section confer, help and advise each other as needed, to get the work done. In other words along with their singular responsibilities he lets his people know that they also have a collective responsibility for the overall performance of the group and the section. He demands and expects of them that they collaborate together - normally unprompted by him to deliver the required work output as a work team in conjunction with their individual work outputs.

Succinctly the main point here is the manager communicates the expectation that the group must work cohesively together and produce the required output when the situation requires it. It is an expectation that he demands to see fulfilled - his people know this - they must work together as a team as needed - that is the standard of work practice required, expected and hence has to be delivered.

**ACTION ITEMS**

⇨ *This requires you to get into the team circle focus as opposed to the task or individual focus. Let your people know that part of their performance will be judged by their ability to work well with their colleagues and peers, to be supportive of them, to see mutual interests and to work co-operatively and positively with them as each occasion demands.*

⇨ *Hold periodic group meetings (at least monthly), identify collective responsibilities and evaluate results and success in terms of the whole unit and not in individual terms*

⇨ *Ensure group goals are included in each person's goals and that they are an important and integral part of the performance appraisal process*

### 3.7.7 *Attune to local and organisational politics and become adept in successfully navigating through politically charged situations*

The individual and manager understands that a political agenda overlays the business agenda. The business agenda tends to be straightforward compared to the political agenda in the sense that an objective and rational review of the factual situation will tend to suffice for the business agenda. Sometimes however, the political agenda can be as or more important than the business agenda. In these instances the effective individual understands he needs to attend to the politics as much as or maybe more so than the business end to

*You Can Do Better!*

make required progress. Some facets of the political agenda he needs to
consider are;

who are the decision makers?

if not directly influence able who needs to be "got onside" to influence the
decision- makers?

What are the needs and interests of the known involved parties?

what power does he have in the situation? e.g. specialist knowledge,
information, specialised skills, resources etc.

what parties are dependent on others?

who will benefit from the decision and equally important who stands to
lose?

who is for the status quo, who is for change, who is undecided and who
can be swayed?

what rapport and relationship if any, has the individual and manager with
the various  parties? etc.

Thus the effective self-manager does not ignore the political agenda but rather
builds his profile by developing his rapport and relationships with the relevant
parties and when he can, builds influence, and networking with powerful
individuals who can help him. In as much as he can, he anticipates interests
and needs and attempts to meet them. In cases of political obstacles he
develops methods to sidestep or outmanoeuvre the obstacles by repositioning

and /or changing his proposals, cultivating like-minded allies who have influence etc. He can also build support by reciprocating favours received and more powerfully, going unrequested out of his way, to help influential others on unrelated activities. In these activities he in a sense, can make deposits into a "networking bank account" which he can then hope to draw on when needed at a later date. *An important rule here is that you have to make deposits first (by helping others) before you can make withdrawals.* The effective manager understands very well that he is more likely to obtain the political assistance he needs from people he knows well or those you have cause to be well disposed to him. Equally well he understands the importance of networking (which is discussed elsewhere) as it is difficult to drum up support from people who don't know you and have no pressing reason to help you. Also worth noting is another important social factor related to networking known as **reach** *- which can be defined as how many people know you and in what context good or bad?*

In summary, the effective individual understands that "where there's people, there's politics" and he is adept in reading political situations and agendas and developing strategies to navigate effectively through the politics. Crucially also, the individual will not try to win over the parties with facts, (i.e. using the business agenda) when he understands that there are significant politics at play, i.e. attend to the politics first and then deal with the business agenda may be the more effective strategy.

## ACTION *ITEMS*

⇨ *Accept the fact that the political agenda can be as or more important than the business agenda. Some individuals particularly those you come from a technical/scientific background can be uncomfortable with this in that in their eyes facts and logical argument are paramount. The reality is that while facts and logic are always important, attention also needs to be directed on people's interests and their influence on those in power especially when major business decisions and changes are being considered.*

⇨ *If necessary read appropriate texts on power and influence and on the fundamentals of politics and what constitutes good practice.*

⇨ *Get to understand as much as you can about the politics at work in your own organisation. As necessary discuss the situation with your boss/mentor-trusted colleague. Listen to and observe the conversations and actions of politically astute colleagues and managers. If possible sit down with them and let them give you their impressions of the politics in action and how they position themselves and address the political issues as needed.*

⇨ *Understand that when major business decisions or changes are to be undertaken the political agenda is likely to be very active. In this situation switch your focus, carefully consider and answer the questions on the facets of this political agenda as they have been outlined above.*

### 3.7.8 *Are an effective net worker, identify and collaborate with significant others*

There is a dependence curve relationship, which shows an individual's dependence on both his boss and his peers over time and is shown below

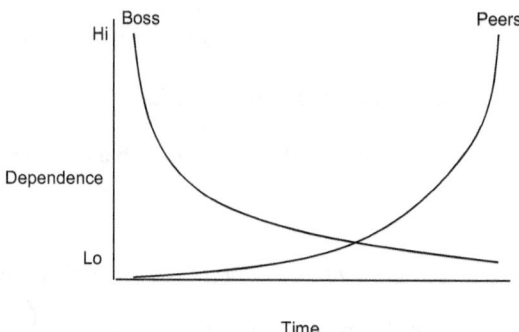

The essential message from the graph is that over time as the individual develops into roles of greater responsibility, his dependence on his boss will decrease while his dependence on his peers will increase over time. As his career develops his collaborative skills become both more necessary and useful as he understands that more and more he needs to involve significant others (people in different company areas and departments) and his peers to get things done and hence be effective in his role.

He understands the need for networking and prospecting for influential people across the organisation and outside the organisation e.g. in clients' organisations. He connects with significant others, developing relationships and building up his network of contacts. As the occasion demands he calls on his contacts to help him get necessary support to get the work done and of course he in turn when asked will reciprocate and provide active help to his contacts to progress their work projects.

## ACTION ITEMS

⇨ *Over time, build your contacts and relationships with a variety of people,*

> *within your business section,*

> *within other business sections,*

> *with different business divisions if appropriate,*

> *with the centralised functions and with business management,*

> *with clients,*

> *with suppliers and outside contractors,*

> *with outside agencies,*

> *with professional bodies etc.*

⇨ *Remember that building a personal network is not a one-time event. You must continue to work on your relationships and keep your network active and up to date. Also your network can be a source of updated and very valuable and useful information, which you might find difficult if not impossible to learn about by other means.*

⇨ *Go out of your way to help and support others on your network whenever you can – you could well need a favour in return some day.*

**Module 7**  │ **Useful Concepts and Tools** │

**There exists** in most of us a strong urge to act quickly in the face of problems, sometimes with limited success. In hindsight we can have cause to regret the rush to action in solving the wrong problem when we should have taken more time to identify the real problem in the 1$^{st}$ place i.e. "the problem is what is the problem? Hence there is a piece to think about on problem solving and framing.

A small section is included on leadership as to its basic implications and what the more effective leadership qualities you may need to develop are.

A section is included on forgetting curves and recalibration of thinking to counterbalance to some extent what was already discussed on learning curves. The important point here is to understand that some learning you may gain has a "best before date" as significant changes in organisations and business management practices occur over the years which render some existing learning and beliefs obsolete, thus requiring new learning to happen.

Finally a section is provided on dealing with difficulties with people, which I think many individuals and managers find challenging for various reasons. This piece does not pretend to be a panacea for all difficulties and ills with people. It does however promote what I believe to be an effective approach, i.e. attack the issue not the person, separate and temporarily dissociate poor attitude/behaviour from the individual personality. This can provide the person

concerned with the necessary space, secure feelings, and confidence to tackle

the problem objectively and dispassionately in tandem with you as the

supporting individual or manager. In a sense it is as if 2 people are openly

discussing and solving attitude/behavioural issues belonging to a separate 3$^{rd}$

party.


## 7.1"The Problem is what is the Problem?"

## Problem Solving, Framing and Reframing

Be very careful how you define a problem because once the problem is defined

then this is the problem that will get solved. This is regardless of the accuracy

or otherwise of the interpretation of the problem and its connection to the

situation in reality.

Another way of looking at it is to say that how you frame a situation will dictate

what gets attention and of course issues that are outside the frame will be

ignored.  Hence the importance of framing and reframing a situation and

inviting healthy debate with others to get a better and fuller understanding of

the situation and the resulting issues that really needs to be addressed.

*You Can Do Better!*

Pictorially this might be represented as follows;

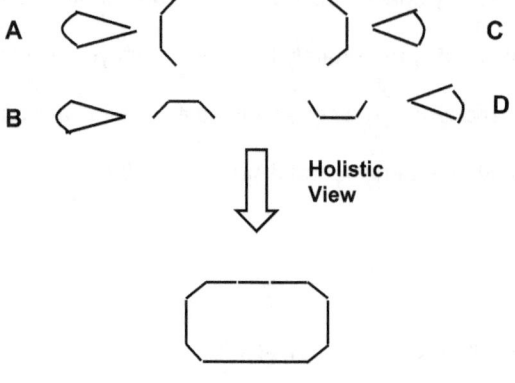

**Real Situation**

i.e. observers A, B,C, and D see different aspects of the situation and through discussion, debate and mutual understanding they can combine all the facets (or viewpoints) together to reveal a more informed picture of the situation in reality. This is ultimately getting to consensus and the so-called holistic view of a situation. Getting here is not easy, as it requires patience, time, discipline, diligence and collaboration by all involved to get to a true interpretation of the situation with all its complicating factors. The above reinforces the point of solving the actual problem, i.e. the problem that exists in reality and not your "preferred" (non- holistic view of the problem) problem to solve.

## 7.2 Leadership and Winning Qualities

Leadership is the ability to influence others to act. Leadership is about making a difference beyond the routine and the status quo. It is also about having followers. So why should people follow you? The answer clearly lies with your knowledge and ability, your good interpersonal skills and of course that you have a script, a positive plan for people to follow, which they can believe in and see, will lead to a better future. Apart from the above what are the most important qualities to have as a leader? Undoubtedly one can list a page long list of qualities of positive character traits and behaviours that could be connected with good leadership.

However if you were to pare it down to an essential short list of say 8 qualities with other qualities seen as nice to have then what would the short list consist of? Below is my take of what is important for a leader – how does this compare with your list?

> ➢ Has a vision for the future – "the man with the plan"
> ➢ Heavily motivated to do different things and make a difference – unhappy and/or bored with the status quo
> ➢ Compulsive and obsessed about making progress against identified actions and projects

> Creative and imaginative to invent new systems, practices, methods and approaches and in overcoming/going around obstacles

> Risk taker and comfortable with exploring new concepts and operating in new unfamiliar areas

> Resilient with a "rubbery" ability to take knocks without being bent out of shape and knocked off course

> Self-reliant – leadership can be a lonely and demanding place to be at times

> Inclusive of people and a natural easy communicator

## 7.3 Lateral Thinking

David Niven the late actor told a good joke one time about a crab. The punch line of the joke was that the crab was walking straight ahead instead of walking sideways as crabs normally do, because the crab was drunk!

So the question is can you think like a crab, i.e. sideways rather than the standard direct route forward approach? Can you sidestep the obvious route, outflank a problem, and think of more insightful and imaginative solutions to a problem. Can you take the contrary view and describe what the problem is not rather than the more usual method of defining what the problem is. By defining and describing what the problem is not, sometimes this gives you a different insight into the parameters and the boundaries of a problem and hence a better insight into novel and innovative ways to solve it.

As an example, one time we were working on a product problem where 2 plastic moulded parts of a product were difficult to separate whereas ease of disassembly was required in use. The crux of the problem was inconsistency in the moulded finish of 1 of the parts. Rather than on fixing on the moulding problem we thought laterally and solved the problem in a different way. We provided "push–off" tabs to the 2$^{nd}$ plastic part thus reducing the problem considerably.

Lateral thinking requires a different type of thinking. It requires thinking from different angles and perspectives and not focusing too much on the problem itself and the perceived constraints therein. Think like you had a magic wand and with one shake you can eliminate the perceived problem. Imagine what would success look like in some detail and then work back towards the original issue. You may find that coming at the problem from a solution end gives you a different perspective and new thinking on the problem leading to novel approaches in its solution.

In the group/team situation lateral thinking may be applied by challenging everyone to come up with the zaniest/craziest solutions and then working on them to fit real world practical methods.

## 7.4 Forgetting Curves and Recalibration of Thinking

In Module 4 the notion of learning curves was described in some detail. Forgetting curves should also exist which would correspond to an exact opposite of the learning curves, i.e. referring back to the shape of the learning curve, the forgetting curve would start with a high knowledge plateau and gradually descend to little or no knowledge, that is the knowledge is forgotten over time.

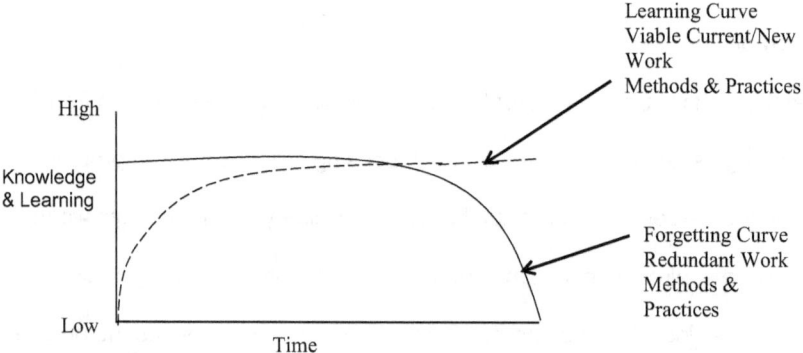

The basic application of this is to understand that some of the lessons you gain over your career need to be forgotten about, as over time they lose their value and eventually no longer apply in the real world. So it is important for you as a manager to shake off outmoded beliefs and practices regardless of how dearly held or comfortable you may be with them. Instead, move with the times and learn about new best current practices, which are now more effective. An example of this would be the gradual shift in management style over the years from the traditional hierarchical and directive approach to the now more required participative and collaborative management style. Hence there is the need over time to reset or recalibrate some of your thinking to maintain the required on-going precision and accuracy of your assumptions and beliefs which are congruent with the existing business environment.

Undoubtedly also, higher managers when faced with a changed environment e.g. deep economic downturn, aggressive competition etc. on occasion will look for sweeping changes in business management style and practices to better cope with the changing environment. This requires flexibility and courage from you as an individual and manager to forget about/unlearn the now outmoded practices (no matter how comfortable you were with them) and adopt new ways of managing yourself and your people as required. As a final point on this it was Einstein who defined madness as people who expect a different result by doing the same things over and over again. Different attitudes and approaches are needed as the environment changes.

## 7.5 Dealing with Difficulties with People

First off you might notice that I chose to use the term "difficulties with people" rather than dealing with difficult people. I think that this is an important distinction to make as avoiding labelling people and attacking the issue and not the person is a more positive and ultimately a more useful approach. The deliberate separation of the difficulty from the person means that the person is likely to feel less threatened, more secure and hence less defensive increasing the chances of a useful discussion and a positive outcome between the person and his manager. Of course there can be a myriad of difficulties you can encounter with people but quite a number can boil down to a few key issues, i.e.

➢ The person is not aware of the problem and the difficulty it is causing

➢ The manager – reportee have mismatched expectations and values

➢ The manager and/or the reportee have unrealistic expectations

Now let's take each issue in turn and see what can be done.

### 7.5.1 The person is not aware of the problem and the difficulty it is causing

This is the situation where the person is blissfully unaware of some flaw in their attitude and /or their behaviour. It can result simply from people in the past not letting the person know in their bid to avoid unpleasantness and cause upset. But now you are the manager of the person and what do you do? High standards apply – you would not speak about the failings of this person behind their back. Hence your only effective recourse is to sit down with the person at a 1-to-1 and address the issue with them. You give the feedback on their failings quoting examples and real instances where possible. You don't talk about the person, don't label them but rather talk about their behaviour and what's lacking which can help to desensitise the issue. For balance you are quick to point out his strengths and what he is good at and why you do appreciate him and the contribution he makes to the business. You explain clearly to the person what altered behaviour you are looking for and what you will do to help him to adjust to the new behaviour. The outcome you want from the 1-to-1 meeting is that the person will reflect on what you have said and the feedback given and will hopefully realise that you are on his side and want to genuinely help him. If this is indeed the case he will internalise the feedback and start working on it. It is the manager's job then to give timely feedback on any progress made and be quick to positively reinforce instances of improved behaviour by encouragement and genuine praise.

### 7.5.2 The manager – reportee have mismatched expectations and values

Again the way to help sort this out is as part of the 1-to–1 meeting process. The manager must clearly communicate as part of the 1-to-1 meeting what his expectations are of the reportee and that the expectations are understood. If this is the case and yet the manager feels that his expectations though reasonable are still not being met then he has a decision to make. Is the reportee not willing or not able to meet his expectations? If it is a question of ability then with added training and coaching the reportee's performance may come up to expectations. If not then the reportee is unable to carry out the role set out for him and either should be transferred to a more suitable position or

else consider his future with the organisation. If on the other hand it is a

question of lack of commitment then the manager needs to dig deeper as to

the reasons for this, e.g. the reportee may be dealing with personal problems

in which case support and counselling over a period may recover the situation.

If this is not the case and the manager has exhausted all reasonable options

with the employee then the manager is duty bound to start the disciplinary

process up to and including removing the employee from the organisation if

needs be.


### 7.5.3 The manager and/or the reportee have unrealistic expectations

In rare instances managers may have unrealistically high expectations of their

reportees. If the reportee himself cannot convince the manager of this then the

manager's boss, HR or an independent business manager needs to become

involved to objectively assess the situation and where warranted, ground the

manager's expectations of his people to realistic levels. This situation is usually

rare and the more common situation is when the employee has an unrealistic

and inflated opinion of his skills and abilities and his ambition tends to race way

ahead of his true learning and development curve and current abilities.

A typical example of this is where the person believes himself to be ready for

significant promotion to higher management levels, senior management or

even general management levels. In reality he may be falling short and struggling with aspects of his current junior management role. To compound the situation he is likely to have held this unrealistic view of himself for some time and nobody has bothered to tackle this difficulty with him.

So what to do? This is similar to the 1<sup>st</sup> situation with the person with a lack of awareness. However in this case this is likely to be a deeper and more chronic problem and hence stronger action is needed, i.e. the use of sympathetic confrontation or put more simply the use of tough love.

The process generally follows the same procedure, i.e. feedback at a 1-to-1 meeting but in this case all the reportee's gaps in performance and lack of ability needs to be listed out clearly and very comprehensively using as many practical/real – life examples as possible along with the resulting limited career prospects that currently realistically follow as a result. While this process may appear brutal it is critical that the reportee is left in no doubt and understands his real performance and abilities assessment. Once the manager sees the beginning of acknowledgement by the reportee of his failings/performance gaps then it is essential that the manager balances this by briefly going over the reportee's good qualities and areas of good performance. The manager can then reinforce the message by providing encouragement about beneficial actions that the reportee can take with the manager's full help and guidance to get to an improved situation. The manager needs to skilfully weave and guide the conversation throughout the 1-to-1 meeting to ensure the message about the reportee's performance and ability gaps is fully communicated and understood, while retaining the reportee's sense of security and confidence with encouragement to begin working on performance gaps.

The use of sympathetic confrontation requires a lot of skill and sensitivity by the manager. When used well it can turn around and re-motivate underachieving employees who will also have more realistic views of themselves and hence will have ambitions better tailored to attainable career plans.

Finally it is important to distinguish between sympathetic and simplistic confrontation. With simplistic confrontation you are really attacking the person full on without any balancing against the person's good attributes and you are clearly not on their side as in sympathetic confrontation. Hopefully as a manager you would only consider using simplistic confrontation as a measure of last resort when all other intervening steps as discussed have been thoroughly tried and failed.

**Module 8**  |  **Practical Insights**

**The inclusion** of a section on practical insights is as a result of speaking with people on the 1$^{st}$ edition of the book where they were looking for me to say something about a number of additional important issues to them and indeed issues that tax most people in their jobs. As a result I have included pieces on meetings, the bane of some people's lives, and recruiting interviews and what might help you to get the right people into your business. There is a piece on senior management and on the central checkpoints involved. The final piece is on change, which is a huge subject so I have focused on a few central change issues around people. There is also a piece on leadership, which is a close twin of change, as you generally can't have one without the other.

## 8.1 Meetings

I remember one time seeing a joke poster about meetings – it went something like this............

Afraid of;

Taking a decision?

Having to do something and being held accountable?

Having to work on your own and achieve something?

Taking personal responsibility?

## *You Can Do Better!*

Rather talk about it than do it?

Then instead why not **hold a meeting**!!

While the above is a somewhat cynical take on meetings it has more than a grain of truth in it. How many individuals, managers included, on occasion 'hide behind' attending interminable meetings! The meetings consist of long drawn out discussion after which minutes are issued and circulated which propose to indicate a veneer of progress. In reality, little is achieved or done and a lot of people's time and organisation resources have been wasted.

The PMA or the Professional Meeting Attender exists in all organisations. Typically they are drawn to meetings like moths to a light. The longer the meetings are the better for the PMA. They can sit for hours at a time, drink plenty of coffee, eat the biscuits, will make vaguely intelligent apposite comments intermittently, nod sagely when higher managers are making a point, and will enthusiastically participate in long theoretical discussions on what might be. The PMA will generally remain silent if there is suddenly some focus and there is a discussion about taking actions and will also be reluctant to bring the meeting to a close – the alternative is he has to go back to his desk and he may actually have to do something! He will also happily sit through long presentations and indeed has sat through numerous PowerPoint presentations of over 100 slides long! After all, he is in a nice warm and dark room, what is there to complain about? Meetings are his comfort zone provided that nobody rocks the boat and pushes for closure, action or assigning responsibility to complete tasks.

Okay, the above is a bit exaggerated but is done so to make an important point - be careful - there is a bit of the PMA in each of us at times.

The golden rule of meetings is that you *greatly limit their number and duration*. Hence as an effective individual and manager you limit as best you can the duration (e.g. through focused agendas, fixed time schedules and good meeting coordination) and the number of meetings that you hold or attend for yourself and encourage your people to do likewise. Why do this? Your success in large measure will be dictated by the time you give to the study and reflection on important business and management issues, devising plans, goals and strategies, carrying them out, monitoring progress and tailoring future actions to what you are learning as you go forward.

Having said all the above there are of course some types of meeting that are vital to have and hence are exceptions to the rule although even here you still need to control their number and duration. In general they are,

- 1-to-1 meetings – which are the basis for setting expectations and communicating at the individual level
- Group communication meetings – unlikely to be held more than once monthly/quarterly

➢ Goal review/strategic review meetings – likely to be held at quarterly
frequency

➢ Project Meetings – by their nature they should be action focused

For the meetings that you do have ensure that the 3 roles of Time Manager,
Commitments Manager (committing people to actions) and Mood Manager
(balanced participation, people have been heard and important issues and
concerns addressed) are carried out. These roles may be done by the one
person e.g. the meeting leader but is not necessarily the case and can be
delegated to other meeting attendees. Also keep an eye on process review
(how well the meeting is going, effective use of group time etc.) as well as the
action review.

So remember, give yourself and your people the necessary space and time to
think, act and ultimately succeed by applying the golden rule of meetings.

## 8.2 Getting the Right Person – Recruitment Interviews
## (In Reverse –Good Questions You Can Be Asked At Interviews)

The first thing to say is that all interviews carry an element of risk in that
despite your best efforts you may get it wrong and hire someone who is not

*You Can Do Better!*

what you wanted or you do not hire someone who was actually good and
suitable.

So how do you minimise the risk? – by asking the right questions, listening well
and paying attention to the interviewee's body language etc. , not interrupting
them and letting them do most of the talking.

You are looking for honesty and as much self-disclosure as you can get from
the interviewee. You are also looking for practical real life examples from the
interviewee, which helps to confirm things for you, rather than parroting back to
you model answers to theoretical or hypothetical situations.

Checkpoints for a promising interviewee are…..

1.  That you like the interviewee as a person
2.  That they have demonstrated as much as they can their practical abilities
    to do the job in question – from qualifications, experience examples and
    range, understanding of technical details and what the job entails
3.  That they are self-motivated, self-disciplined and work to high standards
4.  That they will readily fit into the organisation and business culture
5.  That they are likely to be a future on-going adaptable and growing asset
    to your business

So what are the right questions to ask for a successful interview? The answer
is that there are many that you can use and what follows is a selection of some
of the better questions to ask. Below assumes the obvious questions on

detailing qualifications and professional experience have already been answered.

> ➤ Tell me about the last success you had?
> ➤ Tell me about the last time you failed, and what you learned from it?
> ➤ Tell me 3 things you are most proud of in your career to date?
> ➤ Tell me about a time when you had to overcome a particular challenge?
> ➤ Tell me about a time when you had to persuade or confront someone to get something important done?
> ➤ What has helped make you the person you are today?
> ➤ What people (or events) have most influenced you and what do you most admire about them?
> ➤ Name 3 things that motivate you most?
> ➤ Give me an example of a difficult situation you found yourself in and how you got out of it?
> ➤ Give me an example of how you handle difficult people?
> ➤ If we talked to your best friends what would they say
>
> > i. They particularly admire and like about you?
> >
> > ii. What they do not like about you and would like to change?

*You Can Do Better!*

- Give me a practical example of when you showed particular (pick one)......
    i. Tenacity, hard work, flexibility, adaptability, courage, innovation etc. etc.
- What makes you (pick one).....
    i. Angry, frustrated, impatient, disappointed, motivated, excited etc. etc.
- Give me a practical example of when you worked well in a successful team and what you did in particular to add to the success?
- Give me a practical example of when you helped to overcome team problems?
- How do other people view you do you think?
- Why should we hire you?
- What can you contribute in particular to this business?
- Where do you see yourself in 3 – 5 years' time?
- What are your particular strengths?
- What would you like to change most about yourself?
- Why do you want to work for this organisation?

In conclusion, remember again that it is "Results Through People" and that you are potentially making a major investment on behalf of the business. You need to ensure as well as you can that you are making the best investment by hiring the right person – so take your time, reflect carefully on the answers to questions posed and interviewee feedback. How much good evidence from the interviews do you have to support a hire? Consider carefully the checkpoints above, check with your gut instincts and make your decision.

Now briefly taking the situation in reverse and suppose you are going for interview. Clearly a lot of the material above is very relevant in terms of what interviewers will potentially look for and want from you. In particular be prepared for questions on the type of person you are, what outlook you have and how you deal with problems and challenges. For this to work for you, you need to be able to speak about concrete experiences which demonstrate your good behavioural qualities and performance under pressure. You need to be honest, some self-disclosure is important and hence show a balance by freely admitting to some faults you've had/ mistakes you've made and what you learned from the experience  Be careful though, not to overdo the self-disclosure, as remember you are in the business of selling yourself here; maximising the positive and minimising the negative.

## 8.3 Welcome to Senior Management

One time one of my reports was promoted to a senior management position. As a way to help him I prepared a checkpoint list for him based on my own experience as to what to think about and what might guide him as he grew into his new role. The title of the list was as the above and I hope since that he found it of value in coming to terms with his new position.

The checkpoints are divided into the 3 main areas of management, leadership and self-development as shown below and I think are self - explanatory.

### Leadership Checkpoints

- The only standard is high standards
- Recognise the difference between and the importance of Maintenance and Development
- Sense of perspective – Clarity of thought – What is important / What is a priority
- Having a calming influence
- Why does my boss think/act the way he does – act like your boss
- Results through People
- Delegate, Delegate, Delegate
- Pro-activity – Can Do – A Given

## *You Can Do Better!*

### Management Checkpoints

- Time management

- Continuous focus – on priorities

- Always push for facts – take a $3^{rd}$ party view

- Importance of Goals and Goal Drivers

- Importance of 1-to-1's and periodic Staff Communications

- Let things sit – leave plenty of time for thinking and reflection

- Watch the meetings – reduce and keep very focused

- Action review (What you do) and Process review (How you do it) are both important

### Self-Development Checkpoints

- Self-awareness – emotional intelligence – self control

- Sense of humour and/or ability to laugh at yourself

- Self-Discipline

- Don't take it personally

- Believe in yourself but be yourself – do not get grave, worthy, pompous or arrogant

- Collaborate with your peers and colleagues at all levels in the business  - internal and external to your organisation

*You Can Do Better!*

Do not worry if you disagree with which checkpoints are in which category – it does not matter much - what matters is what each checkpoint is saying to you. Taken as a whole the checkpoints are a snapshot of what good management and leadership is all about and is concise and succinct if not necessarily complete.

A standout point to make here is that as your management role increases, the leadership portion of your role also increases. Hence you can notice a balance between the number of leadership and management checkpoints above and also for that matter the number of self-development checkpoints.

## 8.4 Change

Someone once said, "The art of progress is to preserve order amid change and to preserve change amid order". So you need a routine to maintain order and consistency but also note that change is an imperative as the environment changes. What follows is an eclectic mix of important change issues in particular as they relate to and affect people.

### 8.4.1 Comfort Zones

It used to take me 12 minutes to travel to work every day, which was 6 miles away by car. One day to my horror I noticed the local council had erected an additional set of traffic lights which was on my route. This had the effect of adding 30 seconds or more to my daily journey time. For a week afterwards or so I was annoyed and put out. Why? - Because I was knocked out of my routine and taken out of my comfort zone. Ideally, I guess I was thinking if the lights were not put there, things would go back to "normal" and all would be well. Subconsciously as human beings we are all creatures of habit and are not built to embrace change even though change, small and big is a constant in this world. The past as they say is a different country.

Translating this to the work situation people generally do not like change for the same reason i.e. it knocks them out of their comfort zone even if subsequently the change proves to be for the better. In fact, initially at least they are likely to resist the change. Reverting back to people types as described in Module 4, some 'B' type people or "steady Eddies" as they are termed can have a lot of difficulty coping with significant change. The reason is that they are so aligned and enmeshed in their current routine of work. That being said once you get them over the hump of change and get them active in bedding-in the change they can be excellent doers and implementers on your behalf. Why? - Because knowing that the old routine is definitely gone they will be anxious to set up the new routine and way of doing things and settle into it again as soon as possible (their new zone of comfort). 'A' type people or your high potential people have less difficulty with adapting to change as they are not so engaged with routine. In fact these are the people who will be anxious to be part of the change drive and help you bring it in. An important point though is to ensure that enough 'B' type people are also actively involved i.e. a mix of people is likely to be best for successful change implementation.

So change could be described as jumping from the old and bedding into new comfort zones in response to meeting business environment demands with a sometimes anxious and even scary (for some) transition period in between. Hence ensure that you and your people do not get too comfortable with the existing routine – it will only make the change more difficult when it inevitably comes. In summary, we are creatures of habit and it can be hard to break our habits. Understanding this point, involve your people as much as you can in both designing and implementing the change - although I do not think the council would have me help them erect the new traffic lights! Being actively involved helps people overcome their difficulties with change and reduces their stress and anxiety as they go through it.

Mood management is another important factor in change. You yourself may have "crossed the Rubicon" and have accepted that change must take place. However, why should your people be at that point? When change happens, people can go through a strong and draining emotional process through known phases of shock, then anger, then rejection until finally they feel emotionally prepared to come round to acceptance of the change event. This is based on the bereavement model of change. Therefore, you need to give people some

139

time and space to reflect on and come to terms with impending change. Communicate with them a lot, listen a lot during this time, go out of your way to address legitimate concerns and provide reassurance through on-going progress reviews and communication sessions as the change is being implemented. Also a key point to understand is that if people's mood is low and trust is low then this will make it that more difficult to implement the change. Hence mood management is an important activity in any successful change. A critical point to understand here is not to argue with your people on a rational/logical level when the basis of their problems is actually an emotional one – i.e. mood.

### 8.4.2 The Fat and Happy People

The fat and happy people term is a metaphor used to describe people who live off "the fat of the land". It describes people in your business, who are generally well to highly paid, with good conditions and terms, tend to have a lot of experience and are likely to be your longer serving employees. They are comfortable in doing the jobs they do, are generally not stretched in doing them and have a vested interest in maintaining the status quo as the title suggests. They are in their comfort zone, on the flatter part of the learning curve, are not growing or developing much and hence their contribution to the business is likely to be generally static and not increasing much. Fat and happy people tend to be a subset of the 'B' type or "steady Eddies" classification of employees. By their nature fat and happy people will be resistant to change (think comfort zones again), will be opinionated and will likely due to their experience and length of service have some influence and sway in the organisation – particularly with newer and younger employees.

Hence, I suggest that care needs to be taken that you do not have too high a proportion of fat and happy people as it is not good for your organisation's health, particularly in difficult and rapidly changing business environments. If their number is not managed they can hold you back and delay/block needed organisation change and reform. In this situation a pruning or rationalisation/downsizing to reduce their number and associated costs will be inevitable for the on-going survival of the organisation.

### 8.4.3 Change Constituencies

For any significant change as far as your people are concerned they can be divided into a number of constituencies with respect to the impending change as follows;

- Drivers and Builders
- Supporters
- Sit–on–the-fence people
- Critics
- Destructors

Knowing each type then you deal with each as appropriate to their stance with the change. Simply put you need to nurture and appropriately resource your Drivers and Builders and Supporters constituencies. A campaign of communication and persuasion can work with the Sit–on–the–fence people. Critics need to be listened to; their real concerns addressed and then they should be positively challenged to participate in some active role in the change project. Destructors are clearly against the change and will actively work against it. Hence they need to be either told (instructed if needs be) to adopt a neutral stance to the change and/or else should be transferred into roles where their influence is curtailed from the central core of the operation and they are in effect side-lined at least until such time as the change is successfully implemented.

### 8.4.4 The 10 Absolutes of Leadership

On my various travels across the United States I was one time waiting in someone's empty office waiting to be escorted elsewhere. As I was waiting for some time I looked around the walls of the office at the various plaques etc. and I came across a framed document with the title as above. Having read it I thought it struck true and since I had an impending leadership course to give when I got home I copied it word for word into my notebook. Since then I have used it in a number of leadership training courses and it does cause people to stop and reflect for themselves. The absolutes are as below with some commentary from myself.

- **A Leader is a dealer in hope** – the notion of having a strategy, a positive plan for a better future
- **Leaders know that in times like these there have always been times like these** – the cyclical nature of events, e.g. recession leading to economic growth
- **A boss says 'Go' A Leader says 'Let's Go'** – A good manager is also part of the action
- **A Leader knows that its 'what you learn after you know it all that counts'** – " the more you know, the more you know you don't know"
- **Leaders know that to handle yourself use your head to handle others use your heart** – empathy - "the more I know how I show up for you the more effective I can be"
- **Leaders know that if you lay down with dogs you wake up with fleas** – be careful who you associate with (positive thinkers and doers are better than e.g. cynics)
- **Leaders know that true leadership has less to do with position than it does with disposition** – who you are rather than what your job title says

*You Can Do Better!*

- **A Leader is one who knows the way, shows the way, and goes the way**

- **Leaders know that if you see a snake, just kill it. Don't appoint a committee on snakes** – keep it simple; overcomplicating things just wastes resources and people's time

- **Leaders know that failing does not make you a failure! Giving up and refusing to try again does** – learn from experience, be tenacious and do differently!

**Module 3** | **Behaviours of an Effective Individual and Manager**

## PART 3

**What follows** is the 3r[d] and last part of the effective individual's module with

3 final behaviours detailed

Again the behaviours described below can be prefaced by the word - **YOU**


## 3.8 ARE DECISIVE AND CIRCUMSPECT

meaning...............**YOU.....**

*Take prompt decisions based on getting best information and advice available,*

*Stick by and follow through on resultant actions unless the situation requires*

*course alteration*

*Understand the importance of doing the right thing over being right*

*Are open to all sources of information and take account of all positions prior to*

*decision making*


**Break-Out 3.8 ARE DECISIVE AND CIRCUMSPECT**

**3.8.1** *Take prompt decisions based on getting best information and*

*advice available*

As an effective individual you take a rational and objective approach to

decision making. You collect all the facts and information available to you from

all sources. You understand that you will not have all the information available to be certain of the quality of your decision-making and hence an element of personal judgement is involved. You are also confident enough in demeanour to seek advice when you feel you need it from as appropriate, interested parties, people directly involved or affected, your peers and /or your boss prior to making a decision.

You know that decisions can come from all three areas of your body – your head, your heart and your gut. You understand that in unclear situations you sometimes need to make decisions by going with your gut instincts. You also understand the utility on occasion, of "sleeping on your decision", i.e. reflecting overnight on the jumble of issues which can bring order and clarity to the decision the following day.

You understand the balance needed to prevent rushing a decision (based on inadequate information) and delaying a decision to a degree (wanting all possible information before deciding) that can irretrievably damage the business situation.

Once the decision is taken you stick with it and reviews progress. If however, unfolding events proves the decision to be a wrong one you quickly intervene overturning the decision and set a more appropriate course of action. In other words, you separate yourself objectively from the decision such that it if it has to be overturned or significantly changed you can quickly do so without losing momentum and dealing with unnecessary inner turmoil.

Finally you understand that occasionally you will make wrong decisions. In these instances you will acknowledge your failure, publicly if necessary, will review what went wrong and will take it on board as a valuable learning experience, which will stand you in good stead in the future.

**ACTION ITEMS**

⇨ *Hold in check any tendency you may have to act on impulse and go off "half cocked".*

⇨ *Receive information from a variety of sources if possible and check for compatibility and for emerging trends and issues. Listen to all advice offered. Sift through all the information received and conclude on what you believe to be the most important decision factors.*

⇨ *If at all possible, identify numerous options, weigh them with pros and cons, think about potential solution effects, (i.e. solving one problem but causing another) and identify the most promising option as your decision and proceed.*

### 3.8.2 *Stick by and follow through on resultant actions unless the situation requires course alteration*

As an individual you do not take decisions lightly - you give due consideration to the issues prior to decision-making. Hence once the decision is made you are comfortable with it and focus on the action steps, who to involve etc. and what's needed to implement the decision.

As an individual and manager you are a doer and an achiever and hence naturally you are self-motivated to follow through on resultant actions until they are completed. You are self-assured and confident in what you are doing as on part of this process. However there is one caveat - you do keep an on-going review of the progress (or lack of) made and if necessary are able to make course alterations to the planned actions as you go on. In other words you remain flexible and do not doggedly stick with the original decision if subsequent events prove changes are needed.

**ACTION ITEMS**

⇨ *Having gone through due process it is time to effectively implement your decision and stick by it until the early effects of the outcome are known.*

⇨ *Remain committed until completion of decision implementation. If however, significant adverse impacts are noted, be flexible enough to alter course up to and including reversing the decision if this is needed.*

### 3.8.3 *Understand the importance of doing the right thing over being right*

This speaks again to your view of yourself - your self-esteem, your self-assurance and self-confidence,

- must I always be right?

## *You Can Do Better!*

- Is it possible even to be always right?

The answer is clearly no - hence understand that occasionally you will be wrong and on these occasions you need to be flexible enough and comfortable to admit your position and take an altered course of direction. You do not become unnecessarily deflated on these occasions but take the positives out of it, i.e. the learning and development experience for you.

In unclear and emerging situations sometimes as an individual you are required to take a broad based decision which you know will need to be refined as you get more information and the situation becomes clearer. In such situations you understand that a "ready, fire, aim" approach is required over the more standard "ready, aim, fire" approach in decision-making. This is using the analogy of firing cruise missiles where the precise target is not known or moving until after firing the missile, i.e. decision taken on general course of action refined when specific details become known.

In summary as an effective individual you will always do the right thing even if on occasion this means you have to reverse your original plans and decision.

## ACTION ITEMS

⇨ *Some decisions you make are likely to be wrong and will need changing. Understand this in advance and accept it. Therefore, be prepared to be wrong on occasion and acknowledge it publicly if necessary. Remember you are always bigger than the problem and hence can retreat when it is prudent to do so.*

### 3.8.4 *Are open to all sources of information and take account of all positions prior to decision-making*

As an individual and manager you understand that to make high quality decisions you need as much relevant information as you can get from all sources. It is important that you remain objective and hence avoid attempting to filter information or ignoring parts of the information if it does not support what may be your current prevailing view. You need to be circumspect in listening to relevant advice and making genuine efforts to ensure that you take on board all relevant viewpoints. This does not mean however that the last person you spoke to can sway you in your decision. In other words you retain a balance ensuring that all main factors get equal attention for your judgement. Finally at this stage you must now draw conclusions and judgements as to what factors are most important based on a mental sweep of all the information available to you and then choose the optimal position as you judge it for forward action and take your decision. Once made, you stick with it and implement it. If subsequent events prove that difficulties are arising as a direct result of the decision then as the manager you will revisit it, changing it appropriately to suit the circumstances and promptly move on.

### ACTION ITEMS

⇨ *It is obviously important to remain objective in your decision-making and hence avoid using personal filters and biases - so called selective perception. Take all information in without prior judgement or committing to any position. It is only when all known facts and issues are in from all sources that you are now in a position to determine which are the most relevant factors and what particular information you select and what you filter as part of your considered decision making process.*

## 3.9 ARE A LEARNER AND KNOWLEDGE BUILDER

meaning................**YOU.....**

*Have and grow good grounding and knowledge of the operations of the business and in general management and business principles*

*Show ability to be wrong and are comfortable in being contradicted*

*Continually seek out updated knowledge of your own business and general business environment*

*Periodically update and get updates from staff on current business situation, needs and priorities*

**Break-Out 3.9 ARE A LEARNER AND KNOWLEDGE BUILDER**

**3.9.1 *Have and grow good grounding and knowledge of the operations of the business and in general management and business principles***

Authority flows from the one who knows - so the saying goes. There are 3 sides to knowledge building for you as an individual and manager. The first and most obvious side is the business itself. To immerse oneself in its operations and if possible to work in a few different areas to get perspective on different operating methods, skills used and knowledge of day to day operations. This is the knowledge core but on its own is not sufficient, as working theories or models are also needed for the other 2 sides, i.e.

(1) on management

self-management and people management, the basic principles of management which gives you the necessary foundation to work from in all your personal dealings and in handling yourself well and managing people you are responsible for and

(2) on business principles

You need a working understanding of business and finance from first principles (and not just what happens in your company)

- standard costings, labour rates, overheads build up

- sales revenues, profit margins cost of sales, inventory costs, invoicing, receivables, cash flows etc.

- capital expenditure, return on capital employed, financial reporting and projections etc.

As an effective individual you understand that over time you need to build your knowledge in all 3 areas to increase your effectiveness and ultimately the greater knowledge and understanding you have in all 3 areas the greater the contribution ultimately you will make to the company.

## ACTION ITEMS

⇨ *Take the time and effort necessary to understand in depth the workings of your business section. That is to understand from first principles. This means that if you were to set up the business section tomorrow* from scratch you would know what is needed and what functions are

required. Take the time to ask yourself "why do we do

the things we do and why do we do them the way we do"?

⇒ Take the necessary training courses to gain a broader and deeper

understanding of business, financial and management principles.

⇒ Be curious about how other business sections function, how they

operate and how they fit into the overall business. Ask pertinent

questions of knowledgeable others to broaden your understanding and

ultimately your horizons.

⇒ Look for and take advantage of role change opportunities to new

functions and new areas of the business to gain broader business

knowledge and experience.

⇒ Read appropriately, selecting literature, articles, and books on self and

general management principles and practices. In particular read a

number of books on how proven and successful business people

managed and achieved success in their careers.

**3.9.2 *Show ability to be wrong and are comfortable in being contradicted***

At first glance this is perhaps a strange expression. Who wants to be wrong?

What is meant here is a number of things. As a practising self-manager

through knowledge and experience you will understand and know a lot of

issues surrounding the business. On occasion however, your interpretation will be wrong and it is important that you understand this, i.e. your approach cannot be right all the time and occasionally your colleagues will need to tell you to get you back on track so to speak. Will you accept the feedback? The answer is yes once you understand and are comfortable with the premise that you will not be and could not be right all the time, i.e. welcome to the human race!

In a sense it shows you are fallible on occasion and can be a good thing for your colleagues, i.e. who wants to work with the insufferable manager who is right, or more correctly perceives himself to be right all the time. The key issue here is that you understand that you may be wrong on occasion and hence will be relying on your colleagues to tell you.

You are assured and self-confident in your role and hence such an occasion does not undermine you or your relationship with your colleagues. In actuality you take the whole occasion as a learning experience. Again because of the fact that you will be occasionally wrong, because of your self-assurance people can openly contradict you and you are comfortable with this and do not see it as a personal attack. You understand that people will have opposing views to you on occasion and indeed they may be right in their views.

Therefore you are able to give a measured response exploring the issue (attacking the issue not the person) with the other person to mutually determine what the correct situation is. If indeed you are proven wrong you are quick and generous in acknowledging same with the other person and you move on. You do not dwell on your own occasional failures in interpreting of issues and approach. Rather you learn from them and move on.


**ACTION ITEMS**

➡️ *One definition of assertion is the innate ability to be contradicted. Clearly, a balance needs to be struck between being fully committed to your position when you believe yourself to be right and the ability to back off your position and agree with others when you are shown the right or a better way. Hence, always be prepared to flex your thinking and change course without damage to your ego.*

➡️ *Identify with your ability to change position whilst maintaining your self-confidence and self-esteem. Remember you are always bigger than the problem and hence can move on.*


### 3.9.3 *Continually seek out updated knowledge of your own business and general business environment*

To take effective decisions on on-going business operations you know you need to keep informed and up to date. You understand that the business changes over time and that you need to keep updated on the business, i.e. trends and developments, new issues emerging, competitor activity etc.

*You Can Do Better!*

Apart from obviously keeping abreast of your specific business environment, you will develop and maintain broad background knowledge by informing yourself on the general economy, studying business sections in newspapers and other media and also reading specialist business and finance magazines to broaden your knowledge on the business environment as a whole.

**ACTION ITEMS**

⇨ *Take an active interest in current business activities and trends through attending business update meetings, appropriate business conferences and seminars*

⇨ *Seek out knowledgeable people within the business and ask them about their perspectives on the key issues and trends for the business.*

⇨ *Keep track on current wider business and economic events and trends through diverse reading of business media, newspapers, specialist magazines and the Internet. Subscribe to appropriate business bulletins and magazines.*

### 3.9.4 Periodically updates and gets updates from staff on current business situation, needs and priorities

To ensure the business is being steered in the right direction you as manager must update your staff periodically to keep them well informed and in tune with the business direction and strategy. This is done as part of a regular staff communications process perhaps meetings happening monthly but certainly at least quarterly. Equally well you need to get "bottom up" information from your staff to understand "what's happening at the coalface". This information can be vital to you not only to update you on current details but also to determine whether current business strategies are working and on occasion whether changes in course direction are needed. Again, hopefully this information can be mined as part of the 2 way communications meetings mentioned above.

## ACTION ITEMS

⇨ *Periodically hold informal business and operations communication meetings to update staff on the current position, priorities going forward and challenges and opportunities facing the business. Ensure that the communication is indeed 2-way leaving enough time for staff to ask questions and give feedback on what they are seeing and is of concern to them.*

⇨ *Routinely get out of your office to "take the temperature" on the diverse aspects of the operations and business under your control. Listen to what your people have to say and in particular on your prompting to suggestions and proposals they may have to drive the operation and business forward.*

## 3.10 FORM AND LEAD STRATEGIC ACTIONS

meaning......................**YOU.....**

*Continually survey the environment internally and externally to gain*

*understanding of the overall business position*

*Identify a plan of action to pursue beyond the routine*

*Identify and progress long term goals to protect and strengthen the business*

*Are prepared to take the lead and implement needed change within the*

*organisation and the business*


**Break-Out  3.10 Form and lead strategic actions**

**3.10.1 *Continually survey the environment internally and externally to***

***gain understanding of the overall business position***

As an effective manager you periodically monitor the internal environment by a

range of methods including studying section and consolidated financial monthly

reports noting key movements in expenditure and costs. You will also review

product and or service levels and progress achieved against project schedules.

In particular you are looking out for changed positions (good and bad) with

respect to possible opportunities and current challenges to the business.


For the external environment you will periodically evaluate key business

metrics, revenue, return on income etc. and any emerging trends on same.

## You Can Do Better!

You will monitor competitor activity and assiduously gather client feedback notably on service performance but also on general business trends affecting clients and possible impacts to the business. You will be particularly interested in learning about significant business events and trends and what response the company may need.

In summary you spend time in keeping yourself informed and updated on both internal and external business metrics trends and issues as this keeps you best positioned to respond with timely interventions when and as needed.

## ACTION ITEMS

⇨ *Read appropriate literature and books on business strategy and ensure you gain a broad understanding of the elements of strategy and the need for example for the business to align itself within the business environment it finds itself in.*

⇨ *Develop your own method for evaluating the internal metrics of business and operational performance. (Review literature if necessary on the Balanced Scorecard)*

⇨ *Develop and routinely review key metrics and summary positions for the external view of the business, e.g. profit margins, return on capital, revenues and income per business unit, customer issues and trends, competitor activity, areas of business growth and decline, potential new business opportunities etc.*

*You Can Do Better!*

### 3.10.2 *Identify a plan of action to pursue beyond the routine*

As a good manager you understand the difference and complementary nature of <u>maintenance</u> - retaining the status quo level of business operations and performance and <u>development</u> - developing new business initiatives and methods for improving operations and business performance.

You understand that you must put some time and resource into shaping/reshaping the business model for the future. Hence the action plan you identify must be distinct from achieving more of the same and instead be somewhat creative and innovative bringing new approaches to the business.

Examples of new approaches could be;

- diversifying, by acquiring small growth service business, which provides a good, fit with existing businesses.
- implementing new company-client communication and reporting systems
- customising service levels to suit particular clients etc.
- prospecting for new business ventures, looking at new ways to add value and serve clients

Ultimately you understand that your action plans need to be well thought through and strategic so that by implementing them fundamental differences for the better occur within the business.

### ACTION ITEMS

⇨ *The key point here is that you do some development activity. Dealing*

161

with the day-to-day issues is of course important but is not in itself sufficient. First of all become better informed on the overall strategic position of the business and operations (internally and externally) through the points and actions outlined in the previous section.

➯ From a better-informed position take a decision to pursue one or a few new development activities, possible examples of which are cited in this section.

➯ Remember you don't know what is going to happen with these developments – you are after all exploring new territory. However you can manage the risk by e.g. taking smaller chunks of activity at a time, committing limited funds and setting time limits to review status prior to any further action.

➯ It is difficult to determine how much development activity (versus status quo maintenance activity) you should be doing as it will depend on the particular circumstances of your business and the environment you find yourself in. However, an 80/20 rule split between maintenance and development activities might be a good starting point. The key point to understand is that some development projects need to be progressed to make for a better fit in a changing business environment and to help ensure business continuity into the foreseeable future.

*You Can Do Better!*

### 3.10.3 *Identify and progress long term goals to protect and strengthen the business*

Business strategy is about taking a long-term view of the business and the environment it inhabits and to determine changes that need to be brought about over time to position the business in the best possible footing. It is not so much about the here and now. The emphasis is on the longer term and hence actions taken can be gradual with a slow gestation, they can be multi-step in nature so that progress towards strategic goals builds incrementally over time. Put simply, identifying and acting on strategy is not as straightforward as managing the more familiar and predictable routine operations work and hence requires more thinking and certainly more time. If possible multi-stage performance milestones are set, (i.e. the strategy is broken down into more doable pieces) so that progress can be tracked and that periodic goal reviews to check on-going effectiveness of the strategy are in place.

Examples of specific long-term strategic goals could be;

➢ Reduce service level costs by x % over the next 18 months

➢ Identify and set up a new client business with target revenues of y% of existing revenues in the next 18 months

➢ Reduce headcount costs by z% against budgeted costs by mid next year

➢ Identify and investigate 3 new potential business ventures and pilot the most viable one by year end

163

*You Can Do Better!*

> Carry out customer surveys on the top ten customers; identify at least 2 performance improvement areas where significant gains and benefits can be made and implement action plans for improvement by year end

**ACTION ITEMS**

⇨ *You need to consider the long term as well as the short term. By setting out long-term goals for the business you are forging a business plan into the future. Specific examples of long-term goals are quoted in this section. The important point is that you have long term goals, that they are documented, that they are regularly reviewed (monthly/quarterly) for progress and appropriateness and that goals and activities are modified and/or added in response to on-going environmental signals and business needs.*

**3.10.4 *Are prepared to take the lead and implement needed change within the organisation and the business***

The prerequisite here is that as an effective manager you are well informed and knowledgeable about the business. You also need to be self-assured and confident in your role, as clearly there is an element of risk in taking the lead, doing new things beyond the (safe) routine and changing fundamental aspects of the business and the organisation.

## *You Can Do Better!*

You must have the courage of your convictions, be tenacious and be prepared to see the changes through. Change can be painful and in some cases will be unwelcome and challenged - e.g. due to vested local interests. It is up to you as the manager to face down resistance as needed, to address legitimate concerns, to change attitudes, develop sponsors and identify key people in the organisation who can help bring about the change and finally at this point push for the change.

Leading any change initiatives requires you to be bold, very focused and driven, politically astute to marshal allies and followers around you, sensitive and patient in dealing with genuine concerns and yet ruthless if needs be, in dealing with resistors and those who would block the change.

Some examples of change actions could be;

- ❖ Implementing new/more effective staff performance appraisal systems
- ❖ Introducing new salary and benefit structures
- ❖ Downsizing
- ❖ Improving the quality service culture across the organisation
- ❖ Introducing goal structures with greater accountability for results
- ❖ Eliminating waste and poor work practices across the company
- ❖ Implementing new higher standard procedures
- ❖ Staff rationalisation and re-organisation

*You Can Do Better!*

## ACTION ITEMS

⇨ *All businesses require changing over time. Implementing strategy and long-term goals is also about implementing change. Hence managers must understand change management, the resultant people issues and the ways to bring people along with you in bringing in change. A starting point is for managers to understand change management principles and practices by reading appropriately about them and other people's experience in bringing about successful change in their businesses. There are also numerous change models, which can be useful to managers in their understanding as they are undergoing a change process in their business.*

⇨ *The main success factors for implementing change are to involve your key people in designing and implementing the change (involving the sceptics if you can), frequent progress review, addressing genuine concerns with the change as they arise, and building in appropriate rewards and recognition for people as the elements of the change are successfully implemented*

Module 9    | **10 Strategies For Success** |

**Moses came** back down from the mountain tired after a particularly tough and protracted meeting with God. He sat down among the people and said, "I have good news and bad news. The good news is that I got him down to 10 (Commandments) and the bad news is that number 6 is still in!" (Google it, you Heathen!) The only purpose of the joke above is to stay with the theme of 10, i.e. there are 10 effective individual behaviours as there are 10 modules to this book. Hence when I talk about successful strategies in this module you will not be surprised to know in advance that there are 10 of them. So what follow is a summary discussion and some detail around each strategy.

In culinary terms a "jus" refers to a sauce or gravy that has been boiled continuously to reduce the liquid content and thus concentrates and intensifies the flavours of the sauce. In a similar way if you were to reduce down and synopsize all the relevant and current material on effective approaches to personal career success what would the outcome be? What are the 10 things you need to know to be a success in your career? No doubt this could be the subject of much discussion and debate and hence to cut to the chase I invoke Byrnes's Law which simply states: any hypothesis I invent which I deem to be useful does not need to be proven. As a result below, you will find my interpretation of the necessary ingredients for a successful career for you in terms of strategies that you may want to adopt to advance yourself.

## 9.1 *Deliver More than is Expected*

This might be best explained by your sense of professionalism. Do you aim for a mediocre, good or excellent performance? Your standing in your business will be dictated by your performance and a professional approach demands a good to excellent performance. Delivering consistently more than is expected will get you noticed by the business managers, clients etc. raising your profile which in time will give you opportunities to contribute more to the business at a higher level. Economic Value Added (EVA) is a financial term which means the profit realised in a business over and above the average cost of capital employed in the business. So using this theme when you look at your own contribution how much Contribution Value Added (CVA), contribution above the average (expected amount) do you provide to your business? Key skills you use here are multi–tasking and pace setting. Multi–tasking means progressing your priorities and goals in parallel and effectively *"shuttling"* *between the priorities*, like a juggler keeping a number of balls in the air at the same time. This is much more effective than attending to priorities and goals in sequence as this essentially means you are only able to juggle (progress) one ball (priority or goal) over one period of time. Pace setting means working at an appropriate swift and efficient pace. It could also be described as working with "controlled urgency". Working at a slow pedestrian pace on the other hand will simply not get you goal delivery on or before time.

## 9.2    *Maintain Focus and a High Energy Internal Drive*

Success requires an unwavering focus from you on identifying and acting well on your goals. This requires intensive concentration and deep dedication to the task at hand from you perhaps over long periods of time. You do this in part by self-managing, "block booking" chunks of time for yourself for needed "alone time" and thinking time and assiduously avoiding interruptions during these periods. Along with requiring the mental stamina and steadfastness of purpose to achieve this you also clearly need high personal energy which you can maintain and renew over long periods to deliver well on the necessary goals. Also, show enthusiasm for what you do – it helps to set you apart and acts as a spark for you and others around you to go and Do Better!

**9.3**     ***Broaden and Deepen Your Horizons***

This reflects on your ability to see the "bigger wider picture" as they say rather than concentrating solely on the issues and happenings of your own immediate environment. Be curious and interested about business, management and economic issues that others face across the globe. What are the similarities and differences to your own situation? What different approaches do others use which could have benefits if you used them? Become informed on cultural differences, different approaches and different ways in looking at and dealing with people and business challenges.

**9.4**     ***Develop Your Versatility and Continually Add Strings to Your Bow (Increase your Skill–Set)***

This should be a fairly obvious strategy. Adopt and adapt to a range of different and diverse roles. You need to be in a continuous learning mode always prepared to soak up personal lessons from events and experiences. Clearly as time goes on your skills will need to be updated or at least refreshed – if you get complacent and don't up-skill then your contribution to the business is likely to flat–line and will probably diminish over time. Also of course you need to keep abreast of new technological developments and actively pursue training for yourself in areas which add practical skills that will benefit you and your business as you go on.

## 9.5 *Develop Observational Nous and Attention to Detail*

This is an interesting one, nous referring to the intellect and common sense. Do you have a clear and accurate perception of business performance, events and your environment? What it essentially means is how good you are really as an observer of people, events and data? Hopefully people don't have to stick a placard with a message on it in front of your face before you understand what is going on. You need to have a clear idea about what is going on around you and the nuances that can result from interacting with people, and taking part in business and management activities. When you look at presented data and information can you mine it and extract from it the patterns and trends so that you can both seize the opportunities presented and/or fix the impending business problems that surface from the data? Remember you only have a finite amount of attention to give so make sure that you have clarity about what is happening around you so that you can attend to the right things rather than hoping to stumble on them. Developing attention to detail can help you in the early spotting and fixing of errors, omissions, poor wording and set up, and other detracting issues from written communications and reports, goals and business plans, sales pitches and presentations and financial and operational review reports.

9.6    ***Develop Your Self-Awareness, Social Skills and Sales Skills***

Have that little man/or woman on your shoulder continually, observing on a real time basis the interactions and impact you are having with others. Contain and hold back any dysfunctional or inappropriate impulsive behaviour you may have. ***Get Over Yourself!*** Keep your ego in check, don't feed it and permanently remove it from the field of play. Instead, develop a "real you" style which is positive and that you can be comfortable with. Connect with people and give them your full attention. Wear your empathetic shoes. Show an interest in people, listen a lot more than you talk. Think well of people and they will think well of you. Smile more, show personal warmth and humour. Practise mirroring communication styles (matching body language etc. ;) to align with and fit in with others. Maintain a clear sense of self-respect. Develop a positive self-image, by attending to your personal grooming and maintain a good standard of dress and outward presentation. Always be prepared to sell yourself – identify and play up what you've got and minimise any shortcomings you may have.

9.7       *Be Customer-Focused and Cultivate a Diverse Range of Feedback Sources*

Always, always, always be attuned to identifying and meeting your customers' needs - both external and internal customers. Successful businesses and organisations demand a proactive customer focus which requires you as an individual to possess a strong service ethic. To better serve customers display a positive can-do attitude in all your interactions with them. If you are particularly adept at this you will come more to the attention of business managers and customers alike and your profile within the business is likely to be enhanced.

Cultivating feedback sources refers not just to performance feedback about you but can also be feedback about colleagues around you and the general performance of the business. It is very beneficial to have a range of feedback sources to call on, people in different sections of your business, clients, suppliers, training and business consultants, even competitors. The major point here is that others can help you through their feedback, build a broader, objective and truer picture of your actual performance and your business position. They can even sometimes suggest what options you can pursue to improve your overall performance as an individual and that of colleagues around you and your business as a whole

.

## 9.8 *Stretch Yourself and Maintain the Challenge*

Development and learning come from having to deal with new business, management and operational methods, issues and challenges that are outside of your current realm of experience. This is what stretches you and puts you on an upward slope of the learning curve. Hence welcome new roles, responsibilities and experiences as they help you to stretch and grow. As the poet said "A man's reach should exceed his grasp" or to put it more prosaically ensure your ambition exceeds your current development level. Maintain the challenge simply means continually striving for high standards and high levels of performance for yourself and your business.

## 9.9 *Do More of What You are Good at and Enjoy and Keep Positive*

This is probably obvious but over the years as you develop and grow you become particularly competent and proficient at certain tasks and roles. Also as a general rule you enjoy what you are strong at and excel in. Hence if you can marry the two and position yourself in roles that you are both strong at and enjoy this will lead to a happy fulfilling on–going situation for you.

Also no matter what, maintain a positive personal approach and demeanour and use a positive reinforcement style (think more carrot, less stick) in all your dealings in interacting with and managing people. I can think of no better role model for this than Nelson Mandela with his writing. He spoke about keeping your thoughts positive because they became your words; keep your words positive because they became your behaviour, keep your behaviour positive because it becomes your habits; keep your habits positive because they become your values; and keep your values positive because they become your destiny!

9.10   *Maintain Flexible Thinking, Adapt to Change, Be Creative and Adopt New Approaches to Ride the Waves of Change*

Change is a constant in this world and it is likely that we will need to become more adept at effectively surfing an increasing number of waves of change as time goes on. Welcome change and lean towards it even though your natural inclination is to resist it. Be flexible in your thinking to changing events as they happen to allow you a greater range of responses which will make you more effective in the long run. Tackle the unfamiliar by adopting new approaches and new ways of working and encourage others to do the same.

**Module 10**       | **Last Things** |

**What follows** is a miscellany of observations and ideas in no particular

order. They are based on a reflection of my experience in business as an

individual and in people management over the years. I can't tell you they are

right or wrong, other than to say that they generally worked for me. At least it's

important that you have an awareness of these concepts and ideas and that

you might reflect on the position you take on them.

## 10.1 Management and "Results Through People"

One concise purpose of management is "how to do more with less", i.e. how to

achieve/contribute more to the business with less resources to do so. In

financial terms this could also be described as looking for an increase in the

return on your assets.  Combining this with the "results through people"

philosophy identifies a central business and management obligation, i.e. to

invest in your people. To help them improve, develop, adapt and maximise

their impact and hence contribution to the business. In the final analysis it is

the quality of the people within a business and their on-going ability to

contribute and to adapt to changes in the environment that ultimately will

determine the future success of the business.

## 10.2 Role of good manners

A central theme in all your dealings with people either with individuals or groups at all levels is that you treat them with respect, extending them the necessary courtesies and exercise the use of good manners on all occasions. In any situation regardless of your own personal stress it is never acceptable or wise to be short, rude or disrespectful of anyone.

Ultimately, you will get more from people, have more influence and will generally be more effective and successful in your role if you treat people as equals and with respect. It's all about relationships and rapport building. What about people whom despite your best efforts on your part you cannot come to like or maybe even respect due to e.g. their behaviour? In these cases steer clear of these people as much as possible and limit your dealings with them. There is nothing to be gained in having unnecessary negative experiences or confrontations with these people. It's just a waste of time and can be emotionally draining. Rather, focus on the majority of people, i.e. those who you get on with, and get on with it.

## 10.3 It's not what you say it's what you do

Effective people know they must make a strong connection between their words and deeds. If they say they will do something then they make sure it gets done. Whatever opinions or positions or statements they make will be consistent with their ensuing behaviour. Personal credibility and integrity are at stake here - if you say one thing, then not do it or instead do something different to what was committed, people will become wary of you. If you regularly do not follow up your words or position with consistent behaviour or actions, your standing with others will diminish and people will not trust you. They are unlikely to follow you or take the lead from you, in which case your influence with them is significantly reduced.

Be careful what you say to people, as they tend to take you at your word. They will expect to see a connection and consistency between what you say and what you do! In other words make sure you're publicly stated intentions and commitments translate into action and that the resulting action or behaviour aligns with what you said.

*Remember that you behave yourself into and out of situations – both good and bad.*

Another central point to understand is that ultimately, your reputation is built on what you do and achieve and not what you say. Fine words, intentions and to-do plans are all very well but you will be judged by your deeds.

## 10.4 To like, love, respect or maintain a distance

A question that most managers of people must consider at some time is what is the most appropriate management style to use with their people in terms oftheir closeness and friendliness? To some extent what style you choose can be affected and coloured by the company and the organisation culture you work within i.e. going from extremes of open, informal, friendly, close to more closed formal and coldly professional styles. It will also be affected obviously by your own personal demeanour. So what's right? The style you choose should at least not be at great variance with your company culture but perhaps the best way to put it is as follows; Your people should respect you; Hopefully through your interactions and behaviour towards them they will also like you as a person; loving you, putting you up on a pedestal would be a bit extreme.

Your people and you know you're the boss and know that you have a certain role to play. On occasion you will have to overrule them, give them negative feedback on their behaviour and/or performance and occasionally you may be required to formally reprimand and discipline them. You are not one of them, they hopefully will respect your position and understand you have a job to do - you can't be one of the lads and at the same time be the boss as this lack of consistency would be both confusing and unsettling for your people.

The above suggests an approach to respect, like, probably not love and to maintain a certain distance or separateness to allow you to maintain the high standards necessary. This is why leadership can sometimes be lonely. After that, it's up to you and your particular personality and what you're most comfortable with, in choosing your particular management style with your people.

## 10.5 Can–do

A can-do attitude is a vital part of the effective person's make-up. Some people refer to it as a service ethic that good people have, i.e. that they are here to help, to put themselves out and to contribute.

It is the positive, willing, unselfish, giving of oneself, of some of your time and energy. Business managers who have something important that needs doing, tend to gravitate to those people who display a can-do attitude and hence these people get more development and exposure as a result.

Typically the can-do people are more highly thought of by business management and tend to be favoured as candidates for developmental positions and greater roles within the business as opportunities arise.

Could you be described as a can-do person? On a related point you can turn people around from being negative/complaining by saying "you've told me all about what you can't do - Now tell me what you **can** do" This action tends to refocus people towards a more positive approach.

### 10.6 Taking Ownership

Successful individuals adopt the attitude of owning problems and issues to solve them. They take full responsibility. In effect they act as if they own the business/organisation.

### 10.7 You Can Because You Think You Can

At least up to recently it was said that technically, bumblebees, given their physical size and weight should not be able to fly. Of course the bumblebees being ignorant of this observation continue to fly on regardless! The point here is to be positive in outlook, i.e. I can do this because I think I can. The opposite is if you think you can't do this new thing you certainly won't. So a positive "can do" attitude will get you further in the long run. Remember also that you set the expectation to make a difference for yourself as an individual and your people if you're a manager. Hence "can do" and "you can because you think you can" are 2 core effective attitudes in building your contribution to the business to make a real difference.

## 10.8 Are you Religious or Business-like?

A basic difference between religion and business is that religion is all about effort and business is all about results. The key point in this is that success in business does of course require a certain amount of effort but it must be focused and accurately targeted to get the necessary results. Usually this requires some serious thinking time and reflection by you before you act. The quality of your thinking and planning into the effort you put in is as, or more important than the quantity of effort you ultimately expend. Remember always you have only a certain capacity and finite amount of attention and energy to give. Therefore, regularly check yourself and think; - is this the best use of my time and energy?

## 10.9 Collaborate More, Compete Less

A big question for people as they rise in their careers is how influential they can be with their peers, reports, bosses and business management, clients, customers and outside agencies? In essence this is what leadership ability is all about. So how comfortable are people with you and how prepared are they to get engaged with you, closely working with you, following you and being influenced by you in meeting business goals? Key strengths that influential people have are that they listen well, collaborate well, and are quick to defer to and delegate to others on issues which they know others are better in dealing with. Influential people are humble enough (and smart enough) to defer to others who are more knowledgeable and skilled than themselves on certain issues. In particular a central and very important point here is that as a routine, they actively acknowledge (publicly) the talents and strengths of others in the process of getting the work done. In short, they collaborate rather than compete. Who would you prefer to work with?

## 10.10 The 3 "C"s'

When you have a group of people together and you are looking to mould them into an action oriented effective team the 3 "C"s' model can help you in the process. The 1$^{st}$ C stands for (group) Clarity and this refers back to the piece on problem solving and framing in module 7. Simply put, you need to work with

183

each individual in the group to develop a mutually clear view of what the issues are (and what they're not) to establish real clarity. The $2^{nd}$ C stands for Consensus meaning that after some group discussion of the issues, common ground is reached about the issues and what needs to be done. It is important to note that consensus reaching can involve compromise, not going sometimes with the $1^{st}$ choice of each individual but that each individual can agree and happily go along with and support the actual ideas and solutions chosen. Finally the $3^{rd}$ C is Commitment where actions are clearly defined and assigned in a balanced way across the group, i.e. who will do what by when? It is important to note also that the process needs to happen in sequence to work i.e. you need consensus before you will get real commitment to action and you need to get to group clarity before you can hope to achieve real group consensus and hence mould people into an action-focused mutually supportive team.

## 10.11 Change, Learning Curves and Comfort Zones

People fear and resist change because they are being knocked out of their comfort zone (where they feel secure in their mastery of the routine – think learning curves) into an unsure future. As part of the change transition they are displaced onto a rising slope of their personal learning curve and hence significant growth and development is likely for individuals as they progress through the change process. From this perspective you should perhaps welcome and embrace most change which comes your way as it is likely to help you develop and grow. So, your growth and development could be described as the process of jumping out of your current comfort zone onto a new learning curve until you master the new situation and settle into a new zone of comfort. One final important point to make on implementing change is that there are stages that everyone must go through as part of the change acceptance process. Hence in any change process, individuals are likely to be at different stages and hence different stages of readiness to embrace the change and move on.it is important you recognise this point by giving the individuals enough time and space to effectively surf the waves of change.

## 10.12 Positive Reinforcement

Part of your management role is about selling. It is about selling your goals, concepts and ideas to others. It is about generating real proactive commitment in others rather than passive compliance. In engineering terms the act of pulling is more energy efficient than pushing. So it is with people interactions. "Pulling" people along with you is easier and more effective than trying to push them in front of you. This equates with using a positive reinforcement style i.e. encouraging others, giving praise for good effort, teamwork and performance and inspiring people to take the lead and Do Better!

## 10.13 Sense of humour and sense of perspective

Even in the darkest hours of business when things are going poorly, there are many problems and challenges, recession, maybe even economic depression, and doom and gloom are all around you - remember that it's not life threatening and that these days will pass! On the lighter side a sense of humour is useful and judiciously applied can be effective in relieving tension, making people more at ease with themselves and with the people around them. Sometimes a shared joke, a laugh and the situation becomes more human again when things were looking like they were getting too serious or too ponderous. So humour can lighten the mood when needed, but care needs to be taken that it is used appropriately in the right circumstances and that it is not overdone.

One can get too wrapped up in problems and challenges, rising costs, difficulties with business strategies etc. - on such occasions, mental time out is needed to regain a sense of perspective. Look out the window at nature around you, which does not fret about the last set of monthly accounts and the numbers therein. In the infinity and eternity of all things how big really are the issues you think you are facing? How important are they and how much do they really matter!! Your sense of scale is likely to be too big - time to mentally reset and get a truer sense of perspective.

### *You Can Do Better!*

Maybe you need to take time out, go for a long walk. Concentrate on something non-work related that relaxes you, that you enjoy doing. You need a mental break, rest your mind and focus on something positive, interesting enjoyable, restful. This is the so-called mental bunker time when you need to regroup your thoughts.

Someone once said that 90% of what we worry about never happens. So why do we worry about things that have only a 1 in 10 chance of happening? - get the situation into its true perspective and move on. Sometimes the best thing to do is not to draw conclusions and to delay your response. Sleep on it giving your mind a chance to relax. The next day things won't appear as bad, you are better prepared and your response will be better.

Remember in the infinity and eternity of all things - it doesn't really matter!!

# *You Can Do Better!*

## Role Questionnaire

For each statement below reflect on and decide how much the particular behaviour fits you, between the frequency intervals - never/rarely, sometimes, most times and always. Award 3 points for the best fit, 2 points for the next best fit, 1 point for the next fit and 0 points for the least fit with how often you do the behaviour. Ensure you score each interval. The sum of the 4 frequency intervals will always be 6 points for each behaviour sub category. As always with these questionnaires, be honest with yourself and tell it as it is and not what you think you should be. Remember the purpose is to get a true assessment of yourself, which you can then work on.

|  | Frequency Applies to You | | | |
|---|---|---|---|---|
| **Work to high standards** | Never/Rarely | Sometimes | Most Times | Always |
| Are hardworking | ( ) | ( ) | ( ) | ( ) |
| Demand high standards from yourself and your staff | ( ) | ( ) | ( ) | ( ) |
| Are punctual | ( ) | ( ) | ( ) | ( ) |
| Meet commitments | ( ) | ( ) | ( ) | ( ) |
| Set stretching goals and targets for yourself and your people | ( ) | ( ) | ( ) | ( ) |
| Work hard to eliminate shoddy work and poor work practices | ( ) | ( ) | ( ) | ( ) |
| **Operate by 'results through people' philosophy** | | | | |
| Delegate responsibility readily and effectively | ( ) | ( ) | ( ) | ( ) |
| Drive communication, rapport building and work progress through regular 1–to-1 meetings with all reports | ( ) | ( ) | ( ) | ( ) |
| Demand through your reports that all staff have regular 1-to-1 meetings to drive progress | ( ) | ( ) | ( ) | ( ) |
| Hold a number of goal review meetings throughout the year to evaluate and check progress | ( ) | ( ) | ( ) | ( ) |
| Develop reports to take greater and different work responsibilities | ( ) | ( ) | ( ) | ( ) |
| Use personal authority minimally | ( ) | ( ) | ( ) | ( ) |
| Encourage measured risk taking by reports and focus on learning rather than on mistakes made | ( ) | ( ) | ( ) | ( ) |
| Hold a number of performance reviews with your reports throughout the year | ( ) | ( ) | ( ) | ( ) |
| Actively identify and encourage reports on employee development actions | ( ) | ( ) | ( ) | |
| **Self-manage** | | | | |
| Are an effective time manager | ( ) | ( ) | ( ) | ( ) |
| Continually set/reset priorities and are tenacious in follow through | ( ) | ( ) | ( ) | ( ) |
| Anticipate issues and problems with prompt follow-up to resolve them | ( ) | ( ) | ( ) | ( ) |

## Role Questionnaire – Continued

**Frequency Applies to You**

Never/Rarely   Sometimes   Most Times   Always

**Are achievement oriented**

| | Never/Rarely | Sometimes | Most Times | Always |
|---|---|---|---|---|
| Focus concentration on action planning, progress monitoring and goal completion | ( ) | ( ) | ( ) | ( ) |
| Are single minded and determined in task completion | ( ) | ( ) | ( ) | ( ) |

**Are self-developing**

| | Never/Rarely | Sometimes | Most Times | Always |
|---|---|---|---|---|
| Encourage feedback on your own performance to identify development areas | ( ) | ( ) | ( ) | ( ) |
| Seek out appropriate self-development training for yourself and your staff | ( ) | ( ) | ( ) | ( ) |
| Are proactive in developing your career path | ( ) | ( ) | ( ) | ( ) |

**Are reflective**

| | Never/Rarely | Sometimes | Most Times | Always |
|---|---|---|---|---|
| Are reflective on successes and failures and what to do differently | ( ) | ( ) | ( ) | ( ) |
| Converse with your trusted others on issues to broaden your understanding and to clarify your thoughts | ( ) | ( ) | ( ) | ( ) |
| Think through situations to determine possibilities before deciding on action | ( ) | ( ) | ( ) | ( ) |
| Suspend judgement; maintain flexibility in your thinking in complex/ambiguous situations | ( ) | ( ) | ( ) | ( ) |

**Are personable with social skills**

| | Never/Rarely | Sometimes | Most Times | Always |
|---|---|---|---|---|
| Show genuine and active interest in people | ( ) | ( ) | ( ) | ( ) |
| Operate by relationship 1st, business 2nd rule | ( ) | ( ) | ( ) | ( ) |
| Engender positive working relationships with peers, superiors and reports | ( ) | ( ) | ( ) | ( ) |
| Make regular daily efforts to converse with people 1-to-1 and in groups | ( ) | ( ) | ( ) | ( ) |
| Are comfortable with ability to both lead and be part of teams | ( ) | ( ) | ( ) | ( ) |
| Show ability to develop teamwork and collaborative work ethic amongst work groups | ( ) | ( ) | ( ) | ( ) |
| Attune to local and organisational politics and become adept in successfully navigating through politically charged situations | ( ) | ( ) | ( ) | ( ) |

## Role Questionnaire – Continued

**Frequency Applies to You**

| | Never/Rarely | Sometimes | Most Times | Always |
|---|---|---|---|---|
| Are an effective net worker, identify and collaborate with significant others | ( ) | ( ) | ( ) | ( ) |

### Are decisive and circumspect

| | Never/Rarely | Sometimes | Most Times | Always |
|---|---|---|---|---|
| Take prompt decisions based on getting best information and advice available | ( ) | ( ) | ( ) | ( ) |
| Stick by and follow through on resultant actions unless the situation requires course alteration | ( ) | ( ) | ( ) | ( ) |
| Understand the importance of doing the right thing over being right | ( ) | ( ) | ( ) | ( ) |
| Are open to all sources of information and take account of all positions prior to decision making | ( ) | ( ) | ( ) | ( ) |

### Are a learner and knowledge builder

| | Never/Rarely | Sometimes | Most Times | Always |
|---|---|---|---|---|
| Have and grow good grounding and knowledge of the operations of the business and in general management and business principles | ( ) | ( ) | ( ) | ( ) |
| Show ability to be wrong and are comfortable in being contradicted | ( ) | ( ) | ( ) | ( ) |
| Continually seek out updated knowledge of your own business and general business environment | ( ) | ( ) | ( ) | ( ) |
| Periodically update and get updates from staff on current business situation, needs and priorities | ( ) | ( ) | ( ) | ( ) |

### Form and lead strategic actions

| | Never/Rarely | Sometimes | Most Times | Always |
|---|---|---|---|---|
| Continually survey the environment internally and externally to gain understanding of the overall business position | ( ) | ( ) | ( ) | ( ) |
| Identify a plan of action to pursue beyond the routine | ( ) | ( ) | ( ) | ( ) |
| Identify and progress long term goals to protect and strengthen the business | ( ) | ( ) | ( ) | ( ) |
| Are prepared to take the lead and implement needed change within the organisation and the business | ( ) | ( ) | ( ) | ( ) |

*You Can Do Better!*

## SAMPLE SCORING PLAN

You added up the points in each column for each frequency interval to get a sub total for each behaviour category and you ended up with the points shown.

| Behaviour No. | Behaviour | Max. Points Possible | Never/Rarely | Sometimes | Most Times | Always |
|---|---|---|---|---|---|---|
| 1 | Work to high standards | 36 | 6 | 4 | 20 | 6 |
| 2 | Operate by 'results through people' philosophy | 54 | 2 | 32 | 12 | 8 |
| 3 | Self-manage | 18 | 8 | 8 | 2 | 0 |
| 4 | Are achievement oriented | 12 | 4 | 6 | 2 | 0 |
| 5 | Are self-developing | 18 | 8 | 6 | 4 | 0 |
| 6 | Are reflective | 24 | 12 | 12 | 0 | 0 |
| 7 | Are personable with social skills | 48 | 20 | 12 | 12 | 4 |
| 8 | Are decisive and circumspect | 24 | 1 | 3 | 8 | 12 |
| 9 | Are a learner and knowledge builder | 24 | 6 | 6 | 8 | 4 |
| 10 | Form and lead strategic actions | 24 | 2 | 6 | 14 | 2 |

Your Top 3 scored categories or your strengths are;

- Work to high standards
- Are decisive and circumspect
- Form and lead strategic actions

Your Bottom 3 scored categories or areas for you to work on are;

- Are reflective
- Are personable with social skills
- Self-manage

Work on personal improvement by reviewing the material in the categories where you scored poorly. In particular set specific personal goals for yourself around the accompanying suggested action items

"Play to your strengths and work to remove your weak areas"

*You Can Do Better!*

## References

### Emotional Intelligence

Article: Leadership That Gets Results, by Daniel Goleman - Harvard Business Review - March - April 2000

Workbook: Emotional Intelligence - Mike Fiszer - IMI MSc. In Mgmt. Practice - 2004

Book: Working with Emotional Intelligence, by Daniel Goleman

Book Excerpt: Assertiveness ex. 20 Ways to Manage Better, by Andrew Leigh

Presentation Notes: Emotional Intelligence Competency Framework (Hay) - D.Byrnes Notes - Masters in Mgmt. Practice

Presentation Notes: Success Through Emotional Intelligence - D.Byrnes Notes - Masters in Mgmt. Practice

### Teams and Teamwork

Book: Management Teams: Why they succeed or fail, by Meredith R. Belbin 1981

Extracts: Belbin Team Role Definitions + Questionnaires (source as above)

Extracts: Teambuilding and Leadership - Professional Development Ltd.

Book Excerpt: Building High Performance Teams - ex A Portable MBA in Management – Cohen

Presentation Notes: D.Byrnes – Teams

### Change Management

Book Excerpt: Managing Change - ex A Portable MBA in Management

*You Can Do Better!*

Presentation Notes: D.Byrnes - Leadership and Managing Change

Various Presentation Notes and Change Articles: ex IMI Masters in Mgmt.

**General**

Book: The 7 Habits of Highly Effective People – Covey

Book Excerpt: Power, Politics and Influence - ex A Portable MBA in

Management